Anonymous

Resolutions Passed by the Trustees of Columbia College

from 1874 to 1879

Vol. 2

Anonymous

Resolutions Passed by the Trustees of Columbia College from 1874 to 1879
Vol. 2

ISBN/EAN: 9783337372781

Printed in Europe, USA, Canada, Australia, Japan

Cover: Foto ©Thomas Meinert / pixelio.de

More available books at **www.hansebooks.com**

RESOLUTIONS

PASSED BY THE

TRUSTEES OF COLUMBIA COLLEGE,

FROM

1874 TO 1879.

CONTENTS.

	PAGE
Accumulating Fund	7
Admission	8
Annuity	8
Appointments	8
Appropriations	11
Board of Survey	14
Boat House	14
Building	15
Catalogue	16
Centennial Exposition	17
Clerical Work in President's Office	17
Clerk of Board	17
College of Physicians and Surgeons	18
Committees, Permanent	19
Committee on Site and Removal	19
Compositions, Correction of	21
Degrees	22
Expenditures	24
Extra Allowances	24
Financial	25
Foreclosure of Mortgages	26
Free Tuition	27
Honorary Degrees	28
Instruction	29
Instruction, Course of and Committee on the Course	48
Instruction in Music	50
Inventory of Movable Property	51
Law School, Building	51
Law School, Degrees and Examinations	51

	PAGE
Law School, Faculty	52
Law School, Graduation Honors	53
Law School, Instruction	53
Law School, Registrar	54
Law School, Support of	55
Leases and Rents	56
Leave of Absence	58
Libraries	58
Loss of Coat	61
Observatory	61
Optional Studies	62
Printing	63
Prizes	66
Professorships and Professors	67
Public Worship	72
Repairs and Alterations	73
Resignations	74
Salaries	75
Scholarships and Fellowships	76
School of Mines, Breakage	80
School of Mines, Instruction	80
Servants	85
Sports and Games	86
Statutes	87
Students' Study-Room	87
System of Marking	87
Thanks, Resolutions of	87
Treasurer	90
Tutorships	91
Index	93

TRUSTEES OF COLUMBIA COLLEGE.

RESOLUTIONS

OF THE

TRUSTEES OF COLUMBIA COLLEGE.

ACCUMULATING FUND.

1875, Nov. 1. Appropriation from surplus income.

Resolved, That from the surplus income remaining at the end of the last preceding year shall be appropriated and set apart for the accumulating fund the cash balance, $1,668.12, and $20,951.12 deposited with the New York Life Insurance and Trust Company, with the interest accrued on the last-mentioned amount from the 30th day of September last.

1876, Nov. 6. Resolution on surplus income.

Resolved, That from the surplus income remaining at the end of the last preceding year shall be appropriated and set apart for the accumulating fund—$4,848.35, the cash balance ; $2,000 invested from the general fund in the bond and mortgage of William J. Syms, and $45,731.29 deposited with the New York Life Insurance and Trust Company, with all interest to accrue after the 30th day of September, 1876.

1877, April 2. $5,000 to be added to Accumulating Fund.

Resolved, That five thousand dollars, which has been paid to the Treasurer by the executors of the late John Jones Schermerhorn, as a foundation for scholarships, be added to the accumulating fund.

1877, Nov. 5. Appropriation to Accumulating Fund.

Resolved, That there shall be appropriated to the accumulating fund the cash balance on the 30th September, 1877, $5,281.98, and the amount on deposit that day with the New York Life Insurance and Trust Company, $67,706.92, with the interest on the amount last mentioned from the same day.

1877, June 4. $8,878.40 added to Accumulating Fund.

Resolved, That $8,878.40, heretofore received by the Treasurer for the difference between an award and assessment in the matter of the opening of the Washington Ridge Road, be added to the accumulating fund.

ADMISSION.

1875, March 1.
Requirements for admission to Freshman Class in Greek.

Resolved, That the proposition of the Board of the College to substitute among the requirements for admission to the Freshman Class four books of Xenophon's Anabasis instead of three, and to omit the selections from Jacobs' Greek Reader, is hereby approved.

ANNUITY.

1877, May 7.
Annuity of $2,000 to Prof. Joy.

Resolved, That an annuity of $2,000 be allowed Professor Joy, payable at the usual times, in four equal instalments, to commence on the 15th of August next.

APPOINTMENTS.

1875, Feb. 1.
Geo. Chase appointed Instructor in Law School.

Resolved, That George Chase, Esq., be, and he hereby is, appointed an Instructor in the Department of Municipal Law in the Law School, and that his compensation be fifteen hundred dollars ($1,500) per annum, commencing September 30, 1874, and payable in semi-annual payments, May 15th and November 15th. His duties shall be assigned him by the Warden.

1875, April 5.
Geo. Chase appointed Assistant Professor of Municipal Law.

Resolved, That George Chase, Esq., at present Instructor in the Law School, be, and he is hereby, appointed Assistant Professor of Municipal Law. His duties shall be assigned to him by the Warden of the Law School, and his salary shall continue as heretofore provided, payable, however, hereafter in two equal instalments, on the 15th January and 15th May.

1877, Feb. 5.
Archibald Alexander appointed

Resolved, That Mr. Archibald Alexander be appointed Adjunct Professor of Moral and Intellectual Philosophy, to hold office for the period of three years from the time of entering upon his duties, or during the pleasure of this Board, and to receive a salary at the rate of $2,500 per annum.

1877. Assistant in History and Political Science. *Resolved,* That Richmond M. Smith be appointed Assistant to the Professor of History and Political Science, to hold his office for one year, or during the pleasure of the Trustees, at a salary of fifteen hundred dollars per annum.

1877. May 7. C. F. Chandler appointed Prof. of Chemistry. *Resolved,* That Professor Charles F. Chandler be appointed Professor of Chemistry, to hold his office for three years from the 15th of August next, or during the pleasure of the Trustees.

1877. May 7. Wm. P. Trowbridge appointed Prof. of Engineering. *Resolved,* That Professor William P. Trowbridge be appointed Professor of Engineering, to hold his office for three years from the 15th of August next, or during the pleasure of the Trustees.

1877. June 4. Appointments. School of Mines. *Resolved,* That Henry S. Munroe be appointed Adjunct Professor in Surveying and Practical Mining; William Pistor, Instructor in Drawing; Frederick R. Hutton, Instructor in Mechanical Engineering; Elwyn Waller, Instructor in Qualitative Analysis; Frederick A. Cairns, Instructor in Quantitative Analysis; Pierre de P. Ricketts, Instructor in Assaying; Henry C. Bowen, Assistant in Qualitative Analysis; J. S. C. Wells, Assistant in Quantitative Analysis; F. N. Holbrook, Assistant in Assaying; L. H. Laudy, Assistant in General Chemistry. To hold office severally under the terms of the resolution passed by this Board this day, and that a copy of said resolution be furnished them by the Clerk.

1878. March 4. Resolution appointing G. F. Fisher Registrar of School of Mines at $1.500 per annum. *Resolved,* That George F. Fisher be appointed Registrar of the School of Mines, to hold his office during the pleasure of the Board of Trustees, and to be paid at the rate of fifteen hundred dollars per annum, his duties and salary to begin immediately.

1878. April 1. T. W. Dwight appointed Professor of Law of Contracts, etc. *Resolved,* That Theodore W. Dwight is hereby appointed Professor of the Law of Contracts, Maritime and Admiralty Law, and Warden of the Law School, at a salary, or annual compensation, of fifteen thousand dollars, to commence on the fifteenth day of August, 1878, and to be payable in instalments at the times at which the salaries of the officers of the College are payable. He to hold his office and to be entitled to such compensation during the pleasure of the Trustees;

Resolved, That the Warden of the Law School shall be *ex-officio* a member of the Committee of the Trustees on the School of Law.

1878. May 6. Dr. Ordronaux. Professor of Medical Jurisprudence. *Resolved,* That Dr. John Ordronaux be appointed Professor of Medical Jurisprudence, at a salary of $800 per annum from August 15th, to hold his office during the pleasure of the Trustees.

1878. May 6. Professor Burgess assigned to Chair of Constitutional History, etc., in addition to duties in College. *Resolved,* That Professor Burgess be assigned to the Chair of Constitutional History, and International and Constitutional Law and Political Science in the Law School, in addition to his duties in the College proper, his compensation to continue as now established.

1878. May 6. Professor Geo. Chase appointed Professor of Criminal Law, etc. *Resolved,* That Professor George Chase be appointed Professor of Criminal Law, Torts, and Procedure, at a salary of $3,000 per annum from August 15th, to hold his place during the pleasure of the Trustees.

1878. May 6. Spencer B. Newberry Assistant in Geology in place of W. A. Hooker. *Resolved,* That Spencer B. Newberry be appointed Assistant in Geology in place of W. A. Hooker, to hold office for one year from October 1st, or during the pleasure of the Trustees.

1878. May 6. H. C. Bowen, J. S. C. Wells, F. N. Holbrook, L. H. Laudy. *Resolved,* That Henry C. Bowen, Assistant in Qualitative Analysis; J. S. C. Wells, Assistant in Quantitative Analysis; F. N. Holbrook, Assistant in Assaying; L. H. Laudy, Assistant in General Chemistry, whose terms of office will expire August 15, be severally reappointed to hold office for one year or during the pleasure of the Trustees.

1878. May 6. Reappointment for School of Mines. H. S. Munroe. *Resolved,* That Henry S. Munroe, Adjunct Professor in Surveying and Practical Mining, whose term of office will expire July 1st, be reappointed to hold his office during the pleasure of the Trustees.

1878. May 6. Reappointments in School of Mines. *Resolved,* That William Pistor, Instructor in Drawing; Frederick R. Hutton, Instructor in Mechanical Engineering; Elwyn Waller, Instructor in Qualitative Analysis; Frederick A. Cairns, Instructor in Quantitative Analysis; Pierre de P. Ricketts, Instructor in Assaying, whose terms of office expire August 15th, be severally reappointed, to hold office during the pleasure of the Trustees.

1878, June 3. Richmond M. Smith appointed Adjunct Professor in History, Political Science. etc.

Resolved, That Mr. Richmond M. Smith be appointed Adjunct Professor in History, Political Science, and International Law, at a salary of twenty-five hundred dollars ($2,500) from August 15 next, to hold his office during the pleasure of the Trustees.

1878, Dec. 2. A. L. Holley to deliver a course of ten or twelve lectures to class in iron and steel, metallurgy, etc., at $100 per lecture.

Resolved, That Mr. A. L. Holley, of Brooklyn, be appointed to deliver to the class in iron and steel metallurgy in the School of Mines, as supplementary to the instruction given by the Professor in that subject, a course of ten or twelve lectures on the actual state of the manufacture at the present time, at a compensation of $100 per lecture, said course to be given during the second session of the present year, at such hours as may be designated by the President.

APPROPRIATIONS.

1874, Feb. 2. Appropriation to Department of Mechanics.

Resolved, That the sum of one hundred and fifty dollars be appropriated to the Department of Mechanics and Astronomy, in addition to the appropriation already made for the current year, to defray the expense of transporting the transit instrument from the observatory of Mr. Rutherfurd and remounting it at the College.

1874, April 6. Apparatus for Sewanee University.

Resolved, That the sum of $9.50 be added to the appropriation heretofore made for repairing the apparatus given to Sewanee University, and that a bill of William Grunow of $59.50 for repairing and packing the said apparatus be paid.

1874, May 4. Astronomical Clock.

The resolution to appropriate a sum not exceeding five hundred dollars for the purchase of a clock for the astronomical observatory was, upon the recommendation of the Standing Committee, passed for the second time.

1875, January 4. Regulations for appropriations for maintenance of College, etc.

Resolved, That the following be the regulations under which appropriations made for the maintenance of the College and the School of Mines shall be expended, viz.:

1. All appropriations for the ordinary supplies for the College or School of Mines, for the printing and advertis-

ing for the same, for commencement and exhibitions, for college societies, for sports and games, for physical exercises of the students, and for ordinary repairs, shall be expended under the direction of the President.

2. All appropriations to the Library of the College or to the Library of the School of Mines, shall be expended under the direction of the Library Committee.

3. All appropriations to the Herbarium shall be expended under the direction of the Curator of the Herbarium, with the advice and consent of the President.

4. All appropriations for the benefit of the several departments of instruction in the College and in the School of Mines, shall be expended under the direction of the Professor of the said departments, severally, with the advice and consent of the President; and such expenditures shall be, first, for the necessary repairs, consumption, and other unavoidable contingencies incident to the maintenance of the department in effective operation; and, secondly, so far as there may remain a surplus, for the increase of the apparatus or collections of such department.

5. No bill shall be paid for expenditures out of any of the appropriations above named, until the same shall have been approved by the President ; nor in case of appropriations to the Libraries, the Herbarium and the departments of instruction, until such bill shall have been certified by the proper officer to be correct.

6. All bills for the College, for supplies, for printing and advertising, for repairs and for expenditures for departments of instruction, shall be audited by the Standing Committee before payment, and all bills for expenditures of any kind shall be examined by such committee whenever it shall think proper. It shall be the duty of that committee, as due economy may seem to require, to report any facts and make any recommendations in regard to any of the expenses of the institution.

1876. Dec. 1.
Increase of appropriation for rowing.

Resolved, That an increase of $250 be made to the appropriation for rowing, with the understanding that from this appropriation insurance and ground rent be paid by the Treasurer upon the certificate of the Chairman of the Rowing Association.

1877, June 4. $1,000 appropriated for Practical Mining.

Resolved, That the sum of $1,000, or so much thereof as may be necessary, be appropriated to defray the expenses of a class in practical mining, to be conducted during the ensuing vacation according to the plan submitted to the Board at this meeting, with the approval of the Professor of Engineering.

1877, Oct. 1. Resolution appropriating $7,000 for School of Mines passed and referred to Committee on School of Mines.

Resolved, That a sum not exceeding $7,000 be appropriated to the purchase of instruments necessary for the practical instruction in the field of students in geodesy and surveying, and for other purposes necessary to the efficiency of the course, uch expenditure to be made by the Professor of Engineering under the direction of the President.

1877, Nov. 5. Appropriation of $7,000 for instruction in Geodesy and Surveying.

Resolved, That a sum not exceeding $7,000 be appropriated to the purchase of instruments necessary for the practical instruction in the field of students in geodesy and surveying, and for other purposes necessary for the efficiency of the course, such expenditure to be made by the Professor of Engineering under the direction of the President, to be charged to the Department of Mining and Civil Engineering.

1878, Feb. 4. Resolution appropriating $1,000 for Summer Class in Mining.

Resolved, That there be appropriated the sum of one thousand dollars to defray the expenses of the Summer Class in Mining during the vacation of the summer of 1878, and that the Treasurer be authorized to advance to the Professor so much of the appropriation as may be called for, for the purposes of instruction in the field, to be afterward accounted for by him on production, as far as practicable, of vouchers, and also such amount as may be necessary to defray traveling expenses incurred in making preliminary observations and arrangements.

1878, May 20. Appropriation for new building.

Resolved, That the Trustees present, with the consent of the Board, at their next regular meeting, June 3d, do approve the plans for the new building, and appropriate the sum of $200,000 for its construction, including heating and ventilating apparatus, flagging and grading, and also a new boiler house.

1878, May 20. Committee to make contract for new building.

Resolved, That power be given to the committee or its sub-committee to make contracts in behalf of the College for such construction, apparatus, etc., to which the seal of the College may be affixed.

1878, June 3.
Proceedings of
informal meet-
ing, May 20, ap-
proved, etc.

Resolved, That the proceedings of the informal meeting of less than a quorum of Trustees, held May 20, be approved, ratified and adopted as part of the proceedings of the Board of this day.

BOARD OF SURVEY.

1877, Nov. 5.
Property to be
inspected by
Board of Survey.

Resolved, That at the close of each academic year the property of the College in each department of instruction be inspected by a Board of Survey, who shall report upon the condition of the several objects constituting such property, and declare what, if any, of these have become unserviceable for use, so that they may be properly struck from the inventory of the property of the department.

1877, Nov. 5.
Board of Survey
to consist of
President, Pro-
fessor of De-
partment, etc.

Resolved, That the Board of Survey for each particular department shall consist of the President of the College, the Professor of the Department, and one other officer of instruction, to be designated in each case by the standing committee.

BOAT HOUSE.

1871, Dec. 7.
Appropriation
for Boat House.

· *Resolved*, That it be recommended to the trustees, after an examination by the committee of the plans, to appropriate four thousand dollars towards the cost of a boat-house for the students, provided the balance of the cost of said house be first contributed and paid by the alumni, and with the understanding that such boat-house shall belong to the College for the use of the students, and be under the control and management of the committee organized under the resolutions of this Board, adopted June 3, 1872, for the encouragement of rowing.

Extract from the minutes of the Standing Committee of 11th May, 1875:

1875, May 11.
Conditions on
which appropri-
ation for Boat
House to be
paid.

"At the request of the Treasurer the committee advised that the appropriation toward the cost of a boat-house ought to be paid on the following conditions: That such house shall be completely finished; that the committee organized under the resolutions of the Board of Trustees, passed June 3d and November 4th, 1872, shall certify that all the contracts for building and finishing such house have been duly performed, and that there are no liens or claims against the property; that it is wholly paid for except the sum of four thousand dollars granted by the Trustees, and that it has been placed under the control and management of such committee."

BUILDING.

1874, Jan. 5.
Houses of Professor Joy and Dr. Torrey.

Resolved, That the Treasurer give notice to Professor Joy and to the family of the late Dr. Torrey, that after the first day of May next the houses respectively occupied by them will be required for academic purposes.

1874, March 2.
School of Mines building.

Resolved, That the accommodations for the School of Mines upon the present site be limited to those provided for in the plans prepared and now submitted by the Committee on the Site, and that no more students shall hereafter be admitted into such school than can conveniently be instructed in the rooms assigned by such plans to the several departments.

1874, March 2.
School of Mines buildings.

Resolved, That the assignment made by the same Committee of rooms in the buildings occupied by the undergraduate course be approved and carried into effect, subject, however, to such modifications as may be adopted by such committee.

1874, Nov. 2.
$2,300 expenditure on President's house approved.

Resolved, That the expenditures made by the sub-committee of the Committee on the Site, during the vacation, for repairs to the President's house, the same appearing to have been necessary, be approved, and that a sum not exceeding two thousand three hundred dollars be appropriated to cover the cost of such repairs.

1875, May 3.
Consent to hold meetings in lecture rooms of School of Mines.

Resolved, That the consent of the Trustees be given to the holding of such occasional meetings in the lecture rooms of the School of Mines as may be approved by the President and may not interfere with the hours of instruction or other uses of the building for the purposes of the school.

1875, Dec. 6.
$2,400 appropriated for Hazlett property.

Resolved, That twenty-four hundred dollars ($2,400) be appropriated for the completion and repair of the building

on the Hazlett property, and that the action already taken
by the standing committee on this subject, and the contracts made under their direction for such completion and
repair, be ratified and continued. Also that other contracts
may be made on behalf of this corporation, to which the
seal may be affixed, providing for such completion and
repair.

1878, Nov. 4.
Clerk to sign
and seal appli-
cation to Com-
mon Council for
permission to
erect bay-win-
dow.

Resolved, That the Clerk be authorized to sign and affix
the seal of this corporation to an application on its behalf
to the Common Council of the City of New York for permission to erect and keep a bay window on Madison avenue, in the west front of the new building now erecting for
the undergraduate department.

1879, Jan. 6.
$63,337.14 of the
Accumulating
Fund to be ap-
plied to pay-
ment of cost to
new building.

Resolved, That so much of the accumulating fund as was,
on the first of October, 1878, deposited with the New York
Life Insurance and Trust Company, that is to say, $57,337.14,
together with $6,000, the principal of a bond and mortgage
belonging to the same fund and since that date paid, be
applied to the payment of the cost of the building for the
undergraduate department now in process of erection.

CATALOGUES.

1876, May 1.
Resolution on
number of Cata-
logues.

Resolved, That the edition of the catalogues for the next
year shall be only of the number of copies following:

Of the separate College catalogue.......... 1,500 copies.
Of the separate catalogue of the School of
    Mines............................... 2,000   "
Of the general catalogue................. 500   "

And that no examination papers shall be printed in any of
the catalogues.

1877, Nov. 5.
Number of Gen-
eral Catalogue
increased.

Resolved, That for the present year the number of copies
of the general catalogue to be printed be increased to one
thousand (1,000), and the number of copies of the separate
catalogue of the College be diminished to such an extent
that the appropriation for catalogues shall not be ex-
ceeded.

1878, May 6.
Resolution on
Yearly Cata-
logues.

Resolved, That the yearly catalogues of the several departments shall contain only a list of the several officers, of

the students, with their addresses, of the classes of honor and of the graduates of the year preceding, fellowships, scholarships, and prizes.

1878, May 6. Warden of Law School to issue Catalogues. etc.

Resolved, That the Warden of the Law School shall be at liberty to stitch up for distribution with the catalogue of that school stereotyped matter of information.

CENTENNIAL EXPOSITION.

1876, May 1. To loan models, etc., to Centennial Exposition.

Resolved, That the Professor of Metallurgy be authorized to contribute to the loan collections of models and drawings, now in preparation by the American Society of Civil Engineers for exhibition at the Centennial Exposition, such of the drawings and models belonging to the School as can be spared without inconvenience, the same to be returned in good order after the close of the Exposition.

CLERICAL WORK IN PRESIDENT'S OFFICE.

1879, March 3. President authorized to employ a copying clerk for one month.

Resolved, That the President be authorized to employ a copying clerk for a period not to exceed one month, and at a compensation not to exceed fifty dollars, to assist in the preparation and arrangement of the resolutions of the Trustees passed since 1874, in such form that the same may be printed for the use of the members of the Board.

1879, March 3. Special Committee to report as to an additional clerk for President's office.

Resolved, That it be referred to a special committee of three to inquire and report whether the amount of clerical labor to be performed in the office of the President is not such as to require the appointment of an additional clerk in said office.

CLERK OF BOARD.

1874, June 1. A. Halsey, Clerk pro tem., to sign and seal.

Resolved, That Anthony Halsey be authorized to act as Clerk of this Board, with power to sign and affix the corporate seal to all instruments in writing on the part of this corporation, until the fifth day of October next.

1874, June 1.

Resolved, That the passage of the last preceding resolution shall not operate to prevent the Clerk, William Betts, Esq., from acting in that capacity as heretofore, whenever his health and convenience may enable him so to do.

1874. Nov. 2.
Resignation of
Mr. Betts as
Clerk.

The order of business was suspended to receive from Mr. Betts his resignation as Clerk of the Board. His resignation was accepted. On motion of the Treasurer, it was resolved that the salary of Mr. Betts be paid to the 15th of November.

1874. Nov. 2.
A. Halsey elect-
ed Clerk.

After receiving communications from the Treasurer, the order of business was again suspended, and an election was held to fill the vacancy made by the resignation of Mr. Betts.

Mr. Halsey was then duly elected Clerk.

COLLEGE OF PHYSICIANS AND SURGEONS.

1877. June 4.
Select Commit-
tee on relation
of College of
Physicians and
Surgeons.

Resolved, That it be referred to a select committee to inquire and report whether any change is desirable in the relation of the College with the College of Physicians and Surgeons established by resolutions on this subject, adopted by this Board June 4, 1860. The President, Mr. Ogden, Dr. Agnew, Mr. Rutherfurd, and Mr. W. C. Schermerhorn were appointed the committee.

1878, Nov. 4.
Resolution to
dissolve connec-
tion.

Whereas, The styling the College of Physicians and Surgeons of the City of New York the Medical Department of Columbia College, implies a control by this corporation of the government and system of instruction of the College of Physicians and Surgeons, which control does not exist ; and,

Whereas, In the judgment of this Board, it is inexpedient to continue an academic connection which is only nominal ;

Resolved, That the connection between this College and the College of the Physicians and Surgeons of the City of New York, established by resolutions adopted by this Board on the 4th of June, 1860, be discontinued from and after the   day of   , or from and after some other early day which may be preferred by the College of Physicians and Surgeons ; also,

Resolved, That the Clerk be requested to communicate to the College of Physicians and Surgeons a copy of the foregoing resolution, with the expression of regret of this Board that a careful consideration of the subject at this time has brought this Board to the conclusion that the separation contemplated in such resolution ought to be made.

1878, Nov. 4.
Conference
Committee.

Resolved, That a committee be appointed to confer with the Trustees of the College of Physicians and Surgeons, and learn from them on what terms they will transfer their college to the control of Columbia College as the Medical Department of the latter College.

COMMITTEES, PERMANENT, NUMBER OF.

1875, Jan. 4.
Special Committee on Status of Committees, etc.

Resolved, That a special committee of three be appointed to ascertain the status of the several committees of this Board, and report such scheme as may be advisable to place them on a permanent basis.

1875, April 5.
Resolution on Committees, number, term of service, etc.

Resolved, That at the first meeting of the Trustees, held after the first day of January, 1876, and every third year thereafter, there shall be elected by ballot the following committees :

1st. The Standing Committee, to consist of five members, with Treasurer and Clerk *ex-officio.*

2d. The Committee on the Library, to consist of five members.

3d. The Committee on Honors, to consist of five members.

4th. The Committee on the Course and the Statutes, to consist of five members.

5th. The Committee on the School of Mines, to consist of five members.

6th. The Committee on the School of Law, to consist of six members and Warden *ex-officio.*

Any vacancy occurring by death, resignation, or otherwise, shall be filled for the remainder of the term of the member whose place shall have become vacant.

Three members of any committee shall constitute a quorum. Upon the election of the above committees, all the present committees of the Board shall be discharged.

COMMITTEE ON SITE AND REMOVAL.

1871. March 2.
Committee on Site to make contracts.

Resolved, That the Committee on the Site, or, if authorized by them, their Sub-Committee, have power to approve any contracts for work or purchases proper to be entered into on behalf of this corporation about the erection, making or purchasing the said buildings, alterations, repairs, fixtures, and furniture, and that the Clerk sign and affix the seal to all contracts so approved.

1871. March 2.
Mr. Weeks' house to be vacated.

Resolved, That the Committee on the Site have power to make arrangements for the vacating at an early day of the house now occupied by the janitor, and to make compensation to him for its use until another house can be provided for him by such committee.

1871. Nov. 2.
Compensation for unforeseen work.

Resolved, On the recommendation of the Sub-Committee of the Committee on the Site, that one hundred and twenty-five dollars be paid to John Salisbury, Jr., sub-contractor, for compensation for unforeseen work in the excavation for foundations of part of the buildings recently erected for the School of Mines.

1875. May 3.
Resolution referred to Sub-Committee on Site.

Resolved, That the Sub-Committee of the Committee on the Site be instructed and authorized to make such provision for the security of the overcoats and other property of the students of the School of Mines during their attendance on the school as in their judgment may be proper and necessary.

1876. Dec. 4.
Committee on Removal.

Resolved, That it be referred to a special committee of seven, of which the acting chairman shall be one, to consider and report upon the following subjects : The removal of the site of the institution ; the probable time within which such changes can be effected and the cost it would involve, with the measures proper to provide for such cost ; the expediency of selling or not selling the Wheelock property, and the rules which should, in the opinion of the committee, govern the action of this Board in respect to the erection of new buildings upon the present College grounds.

1877. Jan. 8.
Committee on Removal. Expenses to be paid.

Resolved, That the Treasurer be authorized to pay the expenses which may be incurred by such committee for plans and estimates and other expenses necessary for its information.

The following resolution, offered by the President, was referred to the Standing Committee for consideration and report:

1878. Feb. 4. Resolution on additional accommodations.

Resolved, That it be referred to the same committee to consider and report what measures are necessary, expedient and practicable for providing additional accommodations for carrying on the undergraduate course and the course of the School of Mines.

1878. Feb. 4. No new buildings to be erected.

Resolved, That it is not expedient to enter upon any extended system of erection of new buildings on the present site at this time.

1878. Feb. 4. Report of Committee on Removal.

Resolved, That it is inexpedient to remove the College now to the Wheelock property.

1878. Feb. 4. Report of Committee on Removal.

Resolved, That it is inexpedient to attempt to dispose of the Wheelock property in the present depressed condition of real estate.

1878, April 1. Committee on Removal to have plans and estimates made for building on Madison Avenue.

Resolved, That the Committee on Removal be authorized to have prepared plans and estimates for a new building two hundred feet by about fifty-five feet, to be erected on Madison Avenue, and that they include also an estimate of the additional cost of making a portion of the building fireproof.

1878. May 20. Expense of removal, etc., to be paid by Treasurer.

Resolved, That the expense of the demolition of the west wing and of the removal therefrom of the college property, be paid by the Treasurer, such removal to be made under the direction of the architect with the aid of the College officers.

1878. Dec. 2. Committee on Removal to inquire as to increase of chapel accommodation

Resolved, That it be referred to the Committee on Removal to inquire what increase of chapel accommodation is likely to be necessary from and after the first of October, 1879, and to report to the Board what provision it may deem to be expedient to make in order to secure such increase.

COMPOSITIONS, CORRECTION OF.

1878. Oct. 7. President to employ temporary assistants to correct compositions.

Resolved, That the President be authorized temporarily, until the close of the present year, to employ some competent person to assist in the correction of the compositions of the students, at a compensation not exceeding fifty dollars per month.

DEGREES.

1874. Jan. 5.
Ph.D. applica-
tion of A. H.
Chester.

Resolved, That the conditions of the resolutions of the Trustees concerning candidates for the degree of Doctor of Philosophy, which require that such candidates shall reside at the school while pursuing the studies and investigations prescribed for such degree, be dispensed with in the case of Albert H. Chester, a graduate of the school, now Professor of Physics in Hamilton College, and that he be permitted to complete his said studies and investigations at that college.

1874. April 6.
Proposal for ex-
tension of rule
as to Degree of
Ph.D.

Resolved, That the provisions of the resolution of June 2, 1873, permitting graduates of the School of Mines to become candidates for the degree of Doctor of Philosophy, and fixing the conditions on which such degree shall be conferred, be extended to regular graduates in science of other schools and colleges in good standing legally authorized to grant such degrees, who may become students in our School of Mines for that purpose; and also to professors in our said school who may comply with the conditions of the resolution of June 2, 1873, above cited. Laid over and lost.

1874. Dec. 7.
Degree of Mas-
ter of Laws.

A resolution of this date provides for conferring the degree of Master of Laws. (See INSTRUCTION, Law School.)

1875. April 5.
Permission to
Mr. Waldo to
pursue studies,
etc.

Resolved, That Mr. Leonard Waldo be allowed to pursue a course of study and investigation under the direction of the Faculty of the School of Mines, in accordance with the provisions of the resolution of this Board of June 3d, 1873, and that on the completion of such course to the satisfaction of said Faculty he be admitted to the degree of Doctor of Philosophy.

1877. Jan. 8.
Requirements
for Degree of
Ph.D.

Resolved, That it be referred to the Committee on the School of Mines to report at the next meeting of the Board whether one academic year is not too brief a period for the graduates of the School of Mines, who have pursued a systematic course of higher study under the direction of the Faculty in two or more branches of science, to become eligible for the degree of Doctor of Philosophy; and if, in the judgment of this committee, it is so, to report what period of time and of special study should be deemed a necessary qualification for granting such a degree, and to report any recommendations in regard to such degree.

1878, April 1. Degree of Master of Arts. *Resolved,* That after the annual commencement of June, 1880, the degree of Master of Arts, in course, shall not be conferred except upon Bachelors of Arts of this College, of three years' standing or more, who shall have passed an approved examination upon studies to be prescribed by the Faculty, with the approval of the Trustees ; such examination to be held at some convenient time within the month next preceding each annual commencement.

1878, April 1. Faculty not to examine candidates for A.M. Degree. *Resolved,* That the Faculty of the College shall not be required to conduct the examinations of candidates for the degree of Master of Arts, but that examiners shall be appointed for that purpose by the Faculty, who shall receive compensation for their services from the Board of Trustees.

1878, May 6. Resolution on Degree of Master of Arts as amended. *Resolved,* That the Faculty of the College shall conduct the examinations of candidates for the degree of Master of Arts in such manner and at such times as they shall deem expedient.

1878, May 6. Resolution on Degree of Master of Arts as amended. *Resolved,* That after the annual commencement of June, 1880, the degree of Master of Arts, in course, shall not be conferred except upon Bachelors of Arts of this College, of three years' standing or more, who shall have passed an approved examination upon studies to be prescribed by the Faculty, with the approval of the Trustees.

1879, March 3. Non-resident Candidates for Degree of A.B. *Resolved,* That teachers and others engaged in indispensable occupations which interfere with class hours, may become candidates for the degree of Bachelor of Arts without being held to attendance on class exercises, under the following conditions, to wit :

1. Every such candidate must fully satisfy the requisitions prescribed for entrance to college, and must matriculate as a member of the class which he is found qualified to enter.

2. He must show evidence that the occupation in which he is engaged is one which he cannot relinquish without serious disadvantage.

3. He must pay the usual tuition fee.

4. He must present himself for examination with his

class at the semi-annual examinations, and at such other times as may be appointed by the Faculty.

Such candidates shall be entitled to receive from members of the Faculty such advice and assistance as may be necessary to guide them in their studies.

EXPENDITURES.

1874. Dec. 7.
Expenditure of Appropriations referred to Standing Committee.

Resolved, That it be referred to the Standing Committee to consider and report whether it is expedient to adopt any, and if so what, new regulations to govern the expenditure of appropriations and the approving, auditing, and payment of the bills for such expenditure.

1875. April 5.
Resolution on expenditure.

Resolved, That no expenditure shall be made by any officer of the institution for repairs, alterations, furniture or fixtures, except upon the order of the Trustees or of the Standing Committee, upon a requisition for the same, accompanied by such explanation as shall be necessary, signed by the President, and if to be made in the department of any Professor, signed also by such Professor.

1875. April 5.
Power to Standing Committee.

Resolved, That the Standing Committee shall have authority to order, upon such requisition, from time to time, expenditures for any of the purposes mentioned in the last preceding resolution ; provided, that the cost of all such as shall be authorized at any meeting of the Committee shall not exceed two hundred and fifty dollars ($250).

EXTRA ALLOWANCES.

1878. Jan. 7.
Report of Committee on School of Mines.

The Committee on the School of Mines report that they have considered the application of Professor Newberry (referred to this committee) to be paid the sum of $1,000 for services rendered by him in the academic course, consisting of thirty-five lectures on geology delivered by him to the Senior Class, Professor Joy having been incapacitated by illness from performing this duty, which, with others, belonged to his chair.

1878, Jan. 7.
Resolution
granting $1,000
to Professor
Newberry.

Resolved, That under the peculiar circumstances found to exist in this case, the sum of one thousand dollars ($1,000) be paid to Professor Newberry, as a compensation for his lectures on geology given in Professor Joy's place to the Senior Class last year.

1878, Jan. 7.
Resolution on
application for
compensation
for services.

Resolved, That hereafter this Board will entertain no application from any officer or employé of the College asking for any extra compensation, unless the nature of the service so rendered, and the amount of compensation to be given, shall have been fixed by this Board before the performance of the services so sought to be compensated.

Resolved, That a copy of the last preceding resolution be sent by the Clerk of this Board to each officer and employé of the College.

1879, Feb. 3.
Committee to
order extra com-
pensation to
Professors
Dwight and
Chase.

Resolved, That the Committee on the School of Law have power to order extra compensation to be paid to Professor Dwight and Professor Chase for their temporary discharge of the professorship, not yet filled, of the Law of Real Estate and Equity Jurisprudence.

FINANCIAL.

1874, May 4.
Financial Ordi-
nance amended.

Resolved, That the ordinance of November 26, 1866, establishing a permanent financial policy, be amended by including the provision for the English, classical, and mathematical departments in the number of those of which it is allowable to carry forward the balances unexpended at the end of the year and add them to the appropriations for the year next following.

1874, May 4.
Unexpended
balances.

Resolved, That any balance, which may remain unexpended at the close of the present financial year, of appropriations to the purposes hereinafter named, viz., to the Library of the College, to the Departments of Physics, of Mechanics and Astronomy, and of Chemistry, to the Botanical Library and Herbarium, and to the furnishing of the President's house; also, to the Library of the School of Mines, to the Departments of Analytical Chemistry, of Mineralogy, Metallurgy and the Metallurgical Laboratory, of Mining and Civil Engineering, and of Drawing, and of Geology and Palæontology, be carried forward and added to the appropriations for the same objects for the financial year ensuing.

1875, May 3. Amendment to Financial Ordinance passed. *Resolved,* That the ordinance establishing a permanent financial policy be amended by introducing under the head, "Expenditures for the School of Mines," and within the bracket embracing appropriation, which, if unexpended, may be carried forward and added to the appropriation of the succeeding year, the specifications of "General Chemistry, $500," "of Mathematics, $300."

1875, May 3. Amendment of Financial Ordinance as to expenditures in School of Law. *Resolved,* That the ordinance establishing a permanent financial policy, passed on the 26th of November, 1866, be amended, by the insertion in the allowed expenditures for the School of Law, for the Library $1,250 instead of $1,000, and for the Commencement $750 instead of $250.

1879, June 2. Gebhard Fund to be invested with the general funds of the College. *Resolved,* That the Gebhard fund, amounting to twenty thousand dollars, which was bequeathed by Frederick Gebhard to the corporation to be applied for the endowment of a professorship of the German Language and Literature, and for no other purpose whatever, shall hereafter be invested and kept invested with the general funds of the College, and the income thereof, at the rate of six per centum per annum, shall be applied quarterly to the payment of the salary of the Professor of the German Language and Literature.

FORECLOSURE OF MORTGAGES.

1875, May 3. Sale under foreclosure of premises mortgaged by J.W. Hazlett. *Resolved,* That if, on the sale under foreclosure of the premises mortgaged to this corporation by James W. Hazlett and wife, the same shall be purchased by Joseph W. Harper, William C. Schermerhorn, and Gouverneur M. Ogden, for a sum not exceeding seventeen thousand dollars ($17,000), and the title shall be conveyed to them in fee to hold as joint tenants and not as tenants in common, this corporation will advance to them the purchase money upon receiving from them their mortgage of the said premises to secure the sum advanced without their bond or personal obligation.

Purchase money resolutions May 3, 1875, increased to $18,500.

Resolved, That the limit of the purchase money, mentioned in the resolution of May 3d, 1875, with reference to the sale under foreclosure of the premises mortgaged to this corporation by James W. Hazlett and wife, be increased from seventeen thousand dollars to eighteen thousand five hundred dollars.

FREE TUITION.

Resolution of Aug. 1, 1812, applied to School of Mines.

Resolved, That the provisions of the resolution of August 1st, 1812, exempting the members of the Board of the College from the payment of tuition money for the education of their sons in College, be extended so as to apply to tuition in the School of Mines.

Resolution of June 1, 1868, repealed.

Resolved, That the resolution of this Board, passed on the first day of June, 1868, allowing students under certain circumstances to attend the courses of instruction in the School of Mines free of charge, be repealed.

Sons of President and Professors exempt from tuition fees.

Resolved, That the President and Professors in the service of this corporation shall be exempted from paying tuition money for the education of such of their sons as may from time to time be students in the College or in any school or department under the government of this Board, subject, however, to the existing regulations for the support of the Law School.

Committee on Course and Statutes to inquire as to practical operation of Resolutions of April 3 and Oct. 9, 1865, on free instruction.

Resolved, That the Committee on the Course and the Statutes be instructed to inquire what has been the practical operation of the resolutions of the Trustees of April 3, 1865, and October 9, 1865, allowing students of the College and of the School of Mines to receive instruction free of charge on presenting evidence of their inability to pay the usual tuition fees ; and particularly what has been the average grade of scholarship maintained by the students who have been thus benefited, and in how many instances, if in any, it has happened that young men of more than ordinary ability have been enabled by the assistance thus received to prepare themselves for professions or occupations suited to make them more useful members of society than they would probably otherwise have been ; and that the Committee report to the Trustees whether, in view of the facts thus ascertained, it is in their judgment advisable that the resolutions referred to should be repealed or in any manner modified, and whether free tuition, if granted at all, should not rather be offered as an encouragement to intellectual promise than bestowed as a charity.

1878, April 1 Conditions on which free tui-tion may be granted.

Resolved, That the authority conferred on the President and Treasurer, by resolutions of this Board, of April 3, 1865, and of October 9, 1865, to admit students to the College and the School of Mines free of charge for tuition, be subject hereafter to the following conditions, viz.:

1. No candidate shall be entitled to free tuition who fails to show a proficiency in every subject on which he is examined, expressed by the number 60, the maximum of excellence being understood to be 100.

The candidate for free tuition shall be required to present evidence of his inability to pay the tuition fees.

2. The fact that provision is made by the institution for the free instruction of meritorious students shall be widely advertised.

1878, April 15. Proficiency of candidates for free tuition.

Resolved, That no candidate shall be entitled to free tuition who fails to show a proficiency in every subject on which he is examined, expressed by the number 60, the maximum of excellence being understood to be 100, nor shall he continue to receive free tuition unless in all subsequent annual examinations he shall maintain a standing of 70.

HONORARY DEGREES.

1878, March 4. Degrees of LL.D. and S.T.D.

Whereas, In the view of this Board, the honorary degrees of Doctor of Laws and Doctor in Sacred Theology should be conferred only in recognition of distinguished eminence in the professions to which those degrees properly belong, or in honor of meritorious labors in the field of letters, science, or education ; therefore,

Resolved, That hereafter the name of no candidate for the honorary degree of Doctor of Laws, or Doctor in Sacred Theology, will be considered by this Board, unless the same be accompanied by a written statement of the grounds on which it is claimed that the honor may be justly bestowed ; such statement to be attested by the signature of the proposer, if a member of the Board, or by that of some person of character and standing known to and vouched for by some member or members of the Board; and that all such names, with the accompanying statements, shall be referred without debate to the Committee on Honors, which committee shall consider the same, but shall not report during the meeting at which the nomination is made.

Resolved, That it shall be the duty of the committee to satisfy themselves, before adopting a favorable conclusion, that the candidate is entitled to the distinction proposed on one or the other of the following grounds, viz.:

(1.) That he is the author of some original work of such character as to leave no doubt of the learning, attainments, and literary or professional ability of the writer.

(2.) In addition to other claims to recognition for distinguished ability and learning, he holds an honorable official position in some University, College, or School of Law, Medicine, Theology, or Science of good repute in this country or elsewhere.

(3.) That he is a man of acknowledged high standing or fame in the world of literature or science, involving generally recognized eminence among scholars, jurists, theologians, naturalists, or authorities in exact science.

Resolved, That in case the conclusion is unfavorable, the committee be not required to make any report; but that in case the committee resolve to recommend to the Board to bestow the honor, the report to that effect shall be accompanied by the original testimonials, which shall be subject to be read before the Board, if called for by any member.

COURSE OF INSTRUCTION.

1877, June 4. Course of Instruction.

Resolved, That the distribution of time and subject matter in the instruction of the classes of the College and of the School of Mines, and the duties of the several officers of instruction in the College and the School respectively, be, until the further order of this Board, as hereinafter set forth, viz. :

IN THE COLLEGE.

FRESHMAN CLASS.

FIRST TERM.	SECOND TERM.
Greek Poets,	Greek Historians,
Greek Prose Composition,	Greek Prose Composition,
Greek Prosody,	Latin Prose Writers,
Latin Poets,	Latin Composition in Prose
Latin Prose Composition,	and Verse,
Latin Prosody,	Grecian History,
Grecian History,	Roman Antiquities,
Roman Antiquities,	Algebra,
Geometry,	Rhetoric,
Rhetoric,	English Composition,
English Composition,	Declamation,
Declamation,	German (optional).
German (optional).	

Class instruction in Greek shall occupy three hours per week throughout the year; in Latin, three hours; in Mathematics, five hours; in English Studies, two hours; and in Ancient History and Antiquities, two hours. The time given to German shall be one or more hours per week, as the exigencies of classification may allow. English Compositions shall be criticised privately in presence of their authors. Declamations to take place during the hours assigned to English studies.

SOPHOMORE CLASS.

FIRST TERM.	SECOND TERM.
Greek Poets,	Greek Historians, Orators or
Greek Composition in Prose	Philosophers,
and Verse,	Latin Historians,
Latin Poets,	Roman History,
Roman History,	Grecian Antiquities,
Grecian Antiquities,	Trigonometry (analytical and
Geometry,	spherical),
Trigonometry (plane),	Mensuration,
Chemistry,	Surveying,
Modern History,	Chemistry,
English Literature,	Modern History,
English Composition,	English Literature,
Declamation,	English Composition,
German (optional).	Declamation,
	German (optional).

Class instruction in Greek shall occupy three hours per week throughout the year; in Latin, three hours ; in Mathematics, three hours ; in Chemistry, one hour ; in Ancient History and Antiquities, one hour ; in History and English Literature, three hours ; in Elocution, one hour. The time given to German to be determined by the exigencies of classification. English Compositions to be criticised privately in presence of their authors.

JUNIOR CLASS.

FIRST TERM.	SECOND TERM.
Greek Dramatists,	Greek Philosophers,
Latin Poets,	Latin Ethical Writers,
Composition of Latin Verse,	Composition of Latin Prose,
Analytical Geometry,	Physics—Electricity,
Physics—Doctrines of Heat,	Mechanics,
History,	History,
Logic,	English Classics,
Æsthetics,	General History of Literature,
English Composition,	English Composition,
Declamation,	Declamation,
German (optional).	German (optional).

Class instruction in Greek shall occupy three hours per week throughout the year ; in Latin, three hours ; in Physics, two hours ; in Mathematics, three hours per week during the first term ; in Mechanics, three hours per week during the second term ; in History, two hours per week throughout the year ; and in Logic, Æsthetics, English Literature, and the History of English Literature, two hours per week throughout the year. The time given to German to be determined by the exigencies of classification. English Compositions to be criticised privately in presence of their authors.

SENIOR CLASS.

FIRST TERM.	SECOND TERM.
Required Studies.	*Required Studies.*
Astronomy,	Astronomy,
Physics—Optics,	Physics—Acoustics,
Political Economy.	Political Economy,
Constitutional Government,	Constitutional Government,
Geology and Mineralogy,	Geology and Mineralogy,
English Philosophical Essays.	English Philosophical Essays.

Elective Studies.

Greek Orators or Dramatists,
Latin Dramatists,
Lectures on Latin Literature,
History of Philosophy,
Psychology,
Chemistry,
Calculus,
Physics—Electricity,
German (optional).

Elective Studies.

Greek Orators or Dramatists,
Latin Prose Writers,
Lectures on Greek Literature,
History of Philosophy,
Psychology,
Chemistry,
Calculus,
Physics—Physical Optics,
German (optional).

Class instruction in Astronomy shall occupy two hours per week throughout the year; in Political Science, two hours; in Geology, one hour; in Physics, three hours; and in Philosophy, three hours. In Greek, Latin, the Calculus, and the Higher Physics, as elective studies, the time given to instruction shall be two hours per week for each of these subjects throughout the year. German shall be taught to such extent as the exigencies of classification may allow. English Philosophical Essays to be criticised in presence of their authors.

IN THE SCHOOL OF MINES.

FIRST YEAR.
FOR CIVIL ENGINEERING, MINING ENGINEERING, AND METALLURGY.

FIRST SESSION.

Geometry,
Algebra,
Physics—Doctrines of Heat, viz.: Expansion, Conduction, Radiation, Thermometry, Pyrometry, Latent Heat, Tension of Vapors, Steam.
Chemistry, Inorganic, viz.: the non-metallic elements and their combinations; the alkalies and alkaline earths and their metallic bases; the metals generally, their properties and their compounds.
French,   German,
Drawing, Use of Instruments, Lettering, Topographical and Linear Drawing.

SECOND SESSION.

Algebra,
Trigonometry,
Mensuration,
Physics—Specific Heat, Magnetism, Electricity Static and Dynamic, Thermo-Electricity, Induction, Magneto-Electricity, The Electric Telegraph.
Botany,
French,
German,
Drawing—Machine and Architectural Drawing; Free-Hand Drawing.

FOR GEOLOGY AND PALÆONTOLOGY, AND FOR ANALYTICAL AND APPLIED CHEMISTRY.

The studies pursued shall be the same as in the foregoing, except that, during the second term, Organic Chemistry shall take the place of Trigonometry and Mensuration.

Class instruction in the Mathematics shall occupy four hours per week throughout the year ; in Physics, three hours per week ; in Chemistry, three hours per week ; in French and German, each three hours per week ; in Drawing, one hour per week throughout the year ; and in Botany, two hours per week during the second session.

When not under instruction in the Class-rooms, the students shall be employed during their available hours in practice in the Drawing Academy.

SECOND YEAR.

FOR CIVIL ENGINEERING AND MINING ENGINEERING.

FIRST TERM.
Analytical Geometry,
Descriptive Geometry — plane and spherical projections, warped surfaces,
Surveying, trilinear, triangular and rectangular, with chain, with compass, and with plain-sight angular instruments,
Chemistry, Inorganic,
Qualitative Analysis,
Mineralogy—Blowpipe Analysis,
Zoology,
French,
German,
Drawing—Free-Hand; Mechanical Drawing and Perspective.

SECOND TERM.
Calculus,
Shades, Shadows, and Perspective,
Surveying, trilinear, triangular and rectangular, with chain, with compass, and with plain-sight angular instruments,
Qualitative Analysis,
Crystallography,
Mineralogy,
Zoology,
French,
German,
Drawing — Free-Hand ; Mechanical Problems in Shades, Shadows, and Perspective.

FOR METALLURGY.

The studies pursued shall be the same as in the foregoing, with the omission of Surveying.

FOR GEOLOGY AND PALÆONTOLOGY.

The studies pursued shall be the same as in the foregoing, with the exception of Analytical Geometry, Calculus, Descriptive Geometry, Shades and Shadows, and Surveying, any of which studies, however, may be pursued optionally.

FOR ANALYTICAL AND APPLIED CHEMISTRY.

The studies pursued shall be the same as in Geology and Palæontology, with the addition of Organic Chemistry in the second term.

Class instruction in Analytical Geometry shall occupy three hours per week during the first session ; in Drawing, Descriptive Geometry, and Shades and Shadows, two hours per week throughout the year ; and in the Calculus, four hours per week during the second session. Class instruction in Chemistry shall occupy three hours per week throughout the year ; in Qualitative Analysis, two hours per week ; in Mineralogy, including Blowpipe Analysis and Crystallography, two hours per week ; in Surveying, one hour per week ; in Zoology, one hour per week ; and in French and German, two hours per week, each, throughout the year.

When not under instruction in the Class-rooms, the students shall be employed during their available hours in practice in the Drawing Academy, or in the Laboratory, or in Field Exercise in Surveying.

THIRD YEAR.

FOR CIVIL ENGINEERING.

FIRST SESSION.

Mechanics of Solids, including forces, moments, equilibrium, stability, etc., and elementary machines ; dynamics, including uniform, varied, rectilineal and curvilinear motion, rotation, vibration, impact, work done, etc.

Civil Engineering — general principles, including materials, structures, mechanism, viz.:

    1. Materials — stone, timber, metals, brick, cements, earth, as to (1) composition, (2) strength, (3) durability, (4) mode of preparation, (5) decay and its causes, (6) impurities and defects, (7) tests of quality.

2. Structures—mechanical principles applied to (1) foundations, (2) supports, (3) joints, (4) connecting pieces, (5) stability, strength, and stiffness, (6) carpentry and wooden frames, (7) iron frames, (8) masonry, (9) forces acting on parts of structure and resistance of parts, (10) beams, struts, and ties, (11) factors of safety.
3. Principles of Mechanism, viz.: (1) kinematics, transmission and transformation of motion, (2) elementary combinations in mechanism, (3) link work, bands, gearing, cams, hydraulic connections, pulleys, chains, etc., (4) valve gearing.

Surveying, with chain, with telescopic angular instruments, and with plane table.
Quantitative Analysis.
Mineralogy, Determinative.
Geology, Lithological—rocks and rock masses
Metallurgy (optional)—copper, lead, zinc, tin, the noble metals, etc.
Physics—mechanical theory of heat, electricity.
Drawing—machines, furnaces, plans, free hand drawing.

SECOND SESSION.

Mechanics of Fluids, including pressure, buoyancy, and specific gravities, motion in pipes and channels, undulation, capillarity, tension and elasticity of gases, the atmosphere, the barometer, barometric formulæ, and hypsometry.
Civil Engineering—field work, viz.:
(1) Laying out work in the field, (2) excavations and embankments, (3) railroad curves, (4) setting out tunnels, (5) earthwork, (6) measurement of work, (7) stone cutting.
Surveying, with plane table, with transit compass, and with level, together with instruction in topographic methods.
Physics—physical optics and the undulatory theory of light.
Quantitative Analysis, Stoichiometry.
Mineralogy—Blowpipe Analysis.
Metallurgy (optional)—copper, lead, zinc, tin, the noble metals, etc.
Geology—cosmical, physiographic, and historical.
Drawing—machines, furnaces, and other constructions; free hand drawing.

FOR MINING ENGINEERING.

The topics pursued shall be the same as in the foregoing, except that, in the second session, the topics given below are to be substituted for those under the head, "Civil Engineering," viz. :

Mining Engineering—general principles of the dynamics of machinery, embracing (1) work and resistance, (2) friction in machines, (3) dynamometers and brakes, (4) regulators and governors, (5) efficiency of machinery, (6) strength of parts.

Preparations for Mining, viz. : (1) reconnaissance, (2) boring, (3) sinking of shafts, driving of adits and tunnels, (4) methods and preparations for exterior transportation, (5) buildings and external machinery.

FOR METALLURGY.

The studies pursued shall be the same as in the foregoing, with the omission of Surveying and the topics belonging distinctively to Engineering, and embracing those under the general head "Metallurgy" as compulsory.

FOR GEOLOGY AND PALÆONTOLOGY.

The studies pursued shall be the same as in the foregoing, Mechanics and the Engineering topics being omitted, and the Metallurgical topics and Surveying being made optional.

FOR ANALYTICAL AND APPLIED CHEMISTRY.

The studies pursued shall be the same as in Metallurgy, Mechanics being omitted, and Physics and Geology made optional, and with the addition of the following, viz. :

Applied Chemistry—chemical manufactures, embracing acids, alkalies, and salts, glass, porcelain, pottery, limes, mortars, and cements.

Class instruction in Mechanics shall occupy three hours per week during the first term, and two hours per week during the second ; in Engineering (including both Civil and Mining Engineering), four hours per week throughout the year ; in Quantitative Analysis, one hour per week ; in Stoichiometry, one hour per week during the second session ; in Applied Chemistry, two hours per week throughout the year; in Mineralogy and Blowpipe Analysis, two hours per week ; in Mathematical Physics, two hours per week ; in Geology, three hours per week ; and in Surveying, one hour per week throughout the year.

When not under instruction in the Class-rooms, the students shall be employed during their available hours in practice in the Drawing Academy, or in the Laboratories, or in Field Exercise in Surveying.

During the vacation following the close of this year, the students of Mining Engineering shall be employed in actual work in mines, under the superintendence and direction of the Adjunct Professor of Surveying and Practical Mining.

FOURTH YEAR.

(*Without distinction of Sessions.*)

FOR CIVIL ENGINEERING.

Machines, including prime movers, as driven by (1) animal power, (2) water power, (3) steam, (4) heated or compressed air, (5) the winds ; comprising water wheels, turbines, and reaction wheels, steam engines in their various forms, and air engines.

Principles of Heat applicable to these engines.

Steam Boilers.

Mechanism of Engines.

Machine Tools.

Civil Engineering, embracing (1) foundations, (2) retaining walls, (3) arches, piers, and abutments, (4) bridges and roofs, (5) hydraulic and sanitary engineering, viz. : [1] improvement of rivers, [2] water supply for mills, and for towns and cities, [3] measurement of water supply, [4] flow of water in pipes and canals, [5] sewers and drains—house, surface, and subsoil drainage, [6] ventilation and warming of public buildings.

Surveying with theodolite, principles of geodesy and trigonometrical surveying, underground surveying, and transfer of surveys to surface.

Economic Geology—theory of mineral veins, ores, deposits and distribution of iron, copper, lead, gold, silver, mercury, and other metals ; graphite, coal, lignite, peat, asphalt, petroleum, salt, clay, limestone, cements, building and ornamental stones, etc.

Palæontology—systematic review of recent and fossil forms of life.

Metallurgy (optional).

Drawing—project drawings.

FOR MINING ENGINEERING.

The studies pursued shall be the same as in the foregoing, with the omission of the topics under the general head "Civil Engineering," and the addition of the following, viz. :

Mining Engineering—Exploitation, viz. : (1) attack, adaptation of methods to nature of mineral as to hardness, and situation as to depth, (2) miners' tools and their uses, (3) methods of drilling, cutting, and blasting, (4) explosives and their management, (5) interior transportation, (6) hoisting machinery, (7) pumping engines and machinery, (8) ventilation and ventilating machinery, (9) mechanical preparation of ores, or ore dressing, that is, methods employed in reducing ore to a condition yielding metals, or fitting it for smelting, (10) construction of ore dressing machinery, viz., stamps, crushers, shaking tables, sluices, etc., including coal breakers and screens.

Assaying—ores of lead, silver, gold, tin, antimony, copper, nickel, cobalt, and mercury ; and gold and silver bullion.

Metallurgy—general processes, fuel, furnaces, etc.—iron and steel.

Mining Law.

Bookkeeping.

FOR METALLURGY.

The studies pursued shall be the same as in Mining Engineering, with the omission of the topics belonging specially to Engineering and Surveying.

FOR GEOLOGY AND PALÆONTOLOGY.

The studies pursued shall be the same as in Metallurgy, with the omission of Assaying, and the addition of Surveying as optional.

FOR ANALYTICAL AND APPLIED CHEMISTRY.

The studies pursued shall be the same as in Metallurgy, with the omission of Machines, and the addition of the following, viz. :

Applied Chemistry—(1) Fuel and its Applications ; (2) Artificial Illumination—candles, oils, lamps, petroleum, gas and its products : (3) Food and Drink—water, milk, cereals, starch, bread, meats, tea, coffee, sugar, fermentation, wine, beer, spirits, vinegar, preservation of food, tobacco, etc.; (4) Clothing—textile fabrics, bleaching, dyeing, calico printing, paper, tannin, glue, india-rubber, gutta-percha, etc. ; (5) Artificial Fertilizers—guano, superphosphates, poudrettes, etc.; (6) Disinfectants, Antiseptics, Preservation of Wood, etc.

Class-instruction in the Principles, Construction, and Use of Machines and Engines shall occupy two hours per week throughout the year; in Engineering (including Civil and Mining), four hours per week; in Geodesy and Surveying, two hours per week; in Metallurgy, two hours per week; in Economic Geology, two hours per week; in Ore Dressing and Book-keeping, one hour per week; in Applied Chemistry, two hours per week throughout the year; and in Assaying, two hours per week during the first session. Provision shall be made for instruction in Mining Law by a non-resident lecturer.

When not under instruction in the Class-rooms, the students shall be employed during their available hours in practice in the Drawing Academy, or in the Laboratories, or in Field Exercise in Surveying.

During the Second, Third, and Fourth years, there shall be made frequent excursions into the country on Saturdays for Field Practice in Surveying, by parties of students, under the superintendence and direction of the Adjunct Professor of Surveying and Practical Mining.

DUTIES OF OFFICERS.

OF THE PRESIDENT.

It shall be the duty of the President to take charge and have care of the College generally, of its buildings, of the grounds adjacent thereto, and of its movable property upon the same. To see that the course of instruction and discipline in the College and School of Mines prescribed by the statutes is faithfully pursued, and to prevent and rectify all deviations from the same; and in order to the due discharge of these duties he shall be personally present at the College during all the hours allotted to scholastic exercises, and shall visit the class-rooms from time to time, and keep himself informed of the manner in which the classes are taught.

He shall also have authority and it shall be his duty to call meetings of the Faculty, and to give such directions and perform such acts as shall, in his judgment, promote

the interests of the College, so that they do not contravene
the charter, the statutes, the orders of the Trustees, or the
decisions of the Board of the College.

And it shall be his duty, furthermore, to report to the
Trustees annually, at the stated meeting in June, and as
occasion shall require, the state of the College, and the
measures which may be necessary for its prosperity, and
particularly the manner in which the several Professors
and Tutors perform their respective duties.

OF THE OFFICERS OF INSTRUCTION IN THE COLLEGE.

The Jay Professor of Greek shall, personally, give the
class instruction required by the foregoing Scheme in the
Greek Language and Literature to the Senior and Junior
Classes, and with the aid of a Tutor, if necessary, to the
Sophomore Class, amounting, with the classes as undivided,
to eight hours per week, or, with the classes as at present
divided into sections, to twelve hours per week ; and he
shall also devote such time as may be necessary out of class
hours to the examination and criticism of exercises and
compositions in Greek prose and verse. He shall, moreover, from time to time visit the class-room of the Tutor
in Greek during class hours and supervise and direct the
instruction given by that officer.

The Professor of Latin shall be charged with duties iden-
tically similar to those above defined, and occupying the
same amount of time, in giving instruction to the same
classes in Latin Language and Literature ; and shall in
like manner supervise and direct the instruction given by
the Tutor in Latin.

The Professor of Mechanics and Astronomy shall give
the class instruction required by the Scheme in the Calculus
and in Astronomy to the Senior Class ; in Mechanics and
in Analytical Geometry to the Junior Class ; and in
Surveying to the Sophomore Class, amounting, with the
classes undivided, to seven hours per week during the first
session, and eight hours per week during the second. He
shall also have charge of the Astronomical Observatory,
and shall be authorized to form, and, with the assistance
of a Tutor to instruct, volunteer classes of members of the
Senior Class in College, or of the Fourth Class in the School
of Mines, in Practical Astronomy, to be exercised in obser-

vation and instructed in the methods of computation, at hours which shall not interfere with those allotted to their regular studies.

The Assistant in Astronomy shall aid the Professor in Astronomical observation, in the care of the Observatory, and in the necessary preparation for his experimental lectures ; and shall perform such other duties proper to his office as the Professor may assign him.

The Professor of Philosophy and English Literature shall give the class instruction required by the Scheme in Psychology to the Senior Class ; in Logic to the Junior Class ; and in English Literature to the Junior and Sophomore Classes; and he shall also superintend the exercises of the Sophomore Class in Elocution ; the whole occupying, with the classes undivided, seven hours per week ; or with the Junior and Sophomore classes in sections, as at present, ten hours per week throughout the year. He shall also examine and criticise the written exercises, compositions, and essays of the Senior and Junior Classes, devoting to this labor such time as may be necessary out of class hours. He shall, furthermore, supervise and direct the instruction given by the Tutor in English, from time to time visiting the class-room of that officer for the purpose.

The Adjunct Professor of Moral and Mental Science shall give the class instruction required by the Scheme in Philosophy and the History of Philosophy to the Senior Class; and shall divide with his principal the instruction in Psychology to the Senior Class, and in Logic and English Literature to the Junior, according to their mutual convenience ; his class duties occupying in all from seven to ten hours per week throughout the year. He shall also aid in the criticism of the written exercises, compositions, and essays of the Senior and Junior Classes.

The Professor of Mathematics shall give, with the assistance of a Tutor, the class instruction required by the Scheme in Geometry, Trigonometry, and Mensuration to the Sophomore Class ; and in Algebra and Geometry to the Freshman Class ; amounting, with classes undivided, to five hours per week during the first session, and four hours per week during the second ; or, with the classes divided as at present, to twenty hours per week during the first session, and nineteen hours per week during the second.

He shall also, from time to time, visit the class-room of the Tutor in Mathematics during class hours, and shall supervise and direct the instruction given by that officer.

The Professor of Physics shall give, personally, the class instruction required by the Scheme in the various branches of Physical Science to the Senior and Junior Classes; amounting, with the classes undivided, to seven hours per week throughout the year.

The Assistant in Physics shall aid the Professor in the care of the physical apparatus, in the arrangement of the lecture room, and in the preparation and performance of experiments; and shall perform such other duties proper to his office as the Professor may assign him.

The Professor of History and Political Science shall give the class instruction required by the Scheme in Political Economy and Constitutional Government to the Senior Class; and in History and the Philosophy of History to the Junior Class; amounting, with classes undivided, to four hours per week throughout the year.

The Gebhard Professor of German shall instruct the volunteer classes which may be formed for the study of the German language, giving to this duty such time as may be necessary, not exceeding five hours per week. He shall also give the class instruction required by the Scheme in Ancient History and in Roman and Grecian Antiquities to the Sophomore and Freshman Classes, amounting, with classes undivided, to three hours per week; or, with classes divided as at present, to eight hours per week; and he shall, moreover, take charge of, examine, and criticise the English compositions of the students of the Sophomore Class.

The Professor of Chemistry shall give the class instruction required by the Scheme in Elementary Chemistry to the Sophomore Class, amounting to one hour per week throughout the year; and also, in Theoretic Chemistry, to such members of the Senior Class as may elect that study, who may attend three hours per week with the Second Class of the School of Mines.

The Assistant in General Chemistry shall aid the Professor in the care of the chemical apparatus, in the arrangement of the lecture-table, and in the preparation and performance of experiments; and shall perform such other duties proper to his office as the Professor may assign him.

The Professor of Geology shall give the class instruction required by the Scheme in Geology and Mineralogy to the Senior Class, amounting to one hour per week throughout the year; and also in Lithology, General Geology, and Palæontology to such members of the same class as may elect those studies, who may attend three hours per week with the Third Class of the School of Mines.

The several Tutors shall give instruction in such subjects and at such hours as may be assigned them by the Faculty, in the several departments to which they are attached, to the Freshman, or Freshman and Sophomore Classes. The Tutors in Latin and Greek shall, moreover, examine and criticise the exercises and compositions in those languages, severally, of the students of the Freshman Class; and shall aid the Professors in the examination and criticism of those of the Sophomore Class; and the Tutor in English shall in like manner examine and criticise the English compositions of the students of the same class, and shall hear each member of that class declaim at least twice, and more frequently, if practicable, during each session.

OF THE OFFICERS OF INSTRUCTION IN THE SCHOOL OF MINES.

The Professor of Mathematics shall give, with the assistance of a Tutor, the class instruction required by the Scheme in Pure Mathematics to the students of the First and Second Classes, amounting, with classes undivided, to seven hours per week during the first session, and eight hours per week during the second, or, with classes divided as at present, to ten hours during the first session, and eleven hours during the second, making, together with his duties in the College, thirty hours per week throughout the year. He shall also, from time to time, visit the class-room of the Tutor during class hours, and shall supervise and direct the instruction given by that officer.

The Tutor in Mathematics shall give instruction, under the direction of the Professor, in such subjects as may be assigned him, to the students of the First Class.

The Professor of Physics shall give, personally, the class instruction required by the Scheme in the various branches of Elementary and Mathematical Physics to the students of the First and Third Classes, amounting, with classes undivided, to five hours per week throughout the year ; or, together with his duties in the College, to ten hours per week throughout the year, the Third Class in the School attending in General Physics along with the Senior Class in College twice in the week.

The Professor of Mechanics and Astronomy shall give, personally, the class instruction required by the Scheme in Mechanics, to the students of the Third Class, amounting to three hours per week throughout the year ; or, together with his duties in the College, to ten hours per week throughout the year.

The Professor of Engineering shall, personally, give the class instruction required by the Scheme in the general principles of Engineering, in the special methods of Civil and Mining Engineering, and in the Principles, Construction, and Uses of Machines and Engines, to the students of the Third and Fourth Classes, amounting to ten hours per week throughout the year. He shall also supervise and direct the instruction given by the Adjunct Professor in Surveying and Practical Mining, and by the Assistant in Drawing.

The Adjunct Professor in Surveying and Practical Mining shall, under the general direction of the Professor of Engineering, give personally the class and field instruction required by the Scheme in the principles and practice of Surveying to the students of the Second, Third, and Fourth Classes, and in Ore Drilling, and also in Book-keeping, to the students of the Fourth Class ; amounting for class instruction to five hours per week throughout the year. He shall also give, from day to day, such field instruction in the use of instruments and in practical methods of Surveying as the exigencies of the course will allow ; and shall, especially, make frequent excursions with select companies of students into the country for this purpose, when scholastic exercises are suspended, on Saturdays. During the vacation succeeding the close of the Third Year, he shall, moreover, superintend the students who have completed the studies of that year, in practical work in mines.

The Assistant in Drawing shall give, under the direction of the Professor, the class instruction required by the Scheme in Descriptive Geometry, Shades, Shadows, and

Perspective, and in the principles and practice of Free-hand Drawing and Sketching, Topographical Drawing, and Linear and Mechanical Drawing and Coloring, to students of the First and Second Classes, amounting to three hours per week throughout the year. He shall also, when not engaged in the class-room, give practical instruction to the individual students at their desks in the Drawing Academy, giving attendance for that purpose between the hours of ten A. M. and four P. M., daily, throughout the course.

The Assistant in Mechanical Engineering shall, under the direction of the Professor, give practical instruction in the management of Machines and Engines, and in the construction and use of tools, to students of the Third and Fourth Classes, and to others as may be necessary ; and shall also, under the same direction, aid in giving instruction in Drawing and in Surveying.

The Professor of Chemistry shall, personally, give the instruction required by the Scheme in Elementary and Theoretical Chemistry to students of the First and Second Classes ; and in Applied Chemistry to students of the Third and Fourth Classes, amounting to eight hours per week throughout the year ; or, together with his duties in the College, to nine hours per week throughout the year. He shall also supervise and direct the instruction given in Qualitative and Quantitative Analysis and in Assaying, and to this end shall daily visit the laboratories and acquaint himself with the practical work of the students at their tables, devoting to this object not less than five hours per week.

The Instructor in Qualitative Analysis shall, personally, give the class instruction required by the Scheme in that branch to students of the Second Class, amounting to two hours per week throughout the year. He shall also, when not engaged in the class-room, give practical instruction to the individual students at their tables in the Laboratory, giving attendance for that purpose between the hours of ten A.M. and four P.M., daily, throughout the course.

The Instructor in Quantitative Analysis shall, personally, give the class instruction required by the Scheme in that branch to the students of the Third Class, amounting to one hour per week throughout the year ; and, when not engaged in the class-room, shall give practical instruction to the individual students at their tables in the Laboratory, giving attendance for that purpose between the hours of ten A.M. and 4 P.M., daily, throughout the course. He shall also give the instruction required by the Scheme in Stoichiometry to the students of the Third Class ; or that study may be merged, if found convenient, in the course of Theoretical Chemistry given by the Professor.

The Instructor in Assaying shall give, personally, the instruction required by the Scheme in that branch to students of the Fourth Class, amounting to two hours per week during the first session ; and, when not engaged in the class-room, shall give practical instruction to the individual students in their work in the Assay Laboratory, giving attendance for that purpose between the hours of ten A.M. and 4 P.M., daily, throughout the year.

The Assistants in Qualitative and Quantitative Analysis, and in Assaying, shall give personal aid and instruction to the students in their respective laboratories during the hours assigned to them for such work, attending for that purpose from ten o'clock A.M. to four o'clock P.M., daily, throughout the year.

The Professor of Mineralogy and Metallurgy shall, with the aid of an Assistant, give the class instruction required by the Scheme in Mineralogy, Crystallography, and Blow-pipe Analysis to the students of the Second and Third Classes ; and in Metallurgy to those of the Third Class ; and, except so far as may be provided by the appointment of Metallurgic experts as Lecturers, to those also of the Fourth Class ; amounting to eight hours per week, or, in the case last supposed, to six hours per week throughout the year.

The Assistant in Mineralogy shall aid the Professor in giving personal instruction to the students in Blow-pipe practice, attending for that purpose in the Blow-pipe Laboratory two hours per week throughout the year ; shall prepare and arrange the tables for lectures and conferences, and shall perform such other duties proper to his office as may be assigned him by the Professor.

The Professor of Geology and Palæontology shall, personally, give the instruction required by the Scheme in Botany, to the students of the First Class ; in Zoology, to the students of the Second Class ; in Lithology, General

Geology, and Palæontology, to the students of the Third Class ; and in Economic Geology, to the students of the Fourth Class ; amounting to six hours per week during the first session, and eight hours per week during the second ; or, together with his duties in the College, to seven hours per week during the first session, and nine hours per week during the second.

The Assistant in Geology shall aid the Professor in the work of the Geological Laboratory, and in the care of the collections ; shall prepare and arrange the specimens required by the Professor in his lectures ; and shall perform such other duties proper to his office as the Professor may assign him.

The Instructors in French and German shall, personally, give the instruction required by the Scheme in those languages respectively, to the students of the First and Second Classes, amounting, with classes undivided, to five hours per week each, or, with classes divided as at present, to twenty hours per week, each, throughout the year ; and shall examine and criticise, out of class hours if necessary, the written exercises required of the students in French and German composition.

1877, June 4.
Reference to Special Committee on duties of Professor of History, etc.

Resolved, That it be referred to a special committee of three to make such arrangement for the next year in reference to the duties of the Professor of History and Political Science in the undergraduate department as they shall deem expedient, and that, in the meantime, the clause in the scheme of instruction in relation to the duties of that officer in the College be suspended.

1877. Oct. 1.
Professor of History to change order of arrangement of Scheme of Instruction.

Resolved, That the Professor of History and Political Science be allowed to change the order of arrangement assigned by the scheme of instruction to the subjects taught by him, provided that, in his judgment and that of the President, the efficiency of the department may be promoted by such change.

INSTRUCTION, COURSE OF, AND COMMITTEE ON THE COURSE.

1822, June 2.
Notice required of Resolutions affecting course of instruction, etc.

Resolved, unanimously, That no resolution affecting the course of instruction, discipline, or statutes of the College shall hereafter be finally acted upon by the Board without the unanimous consent of the members present, unless notice shall have been given at a previous meeting of the Board.

1877. Jan. 8. Resolution on Commencement referred to Committee on Course, etc. *Resolved,* That it be referred to the Committee on the Course and the Statutes, in consultation with the Board of the College, to consider the propriety of naming an earlier day for commencement than that upon which it is now held.

1877. Jan. 8. Resolution on Adjunct Professor of Moral and Intellectual Philosophy referred to the Committee on Course, etc. *Resolved,* That it be referred to the Committee on the Course and the Statutes to consider the propriety of appointing an Adjunct Professor in the department of Moral and Intellectual Philosophy.

1877. Feb. 5. Resolution on Department of Christian Evidences referred to Committee on Course. *Resolved,* That it be referred to the Committee on the Course and the Statutes to consider and report upon the propriety of establishing in the College a department of Christian Evidences.

1877. Feb. 5. Resolution on Department of Philosophy of Charity and Correction. *Resolved,* That it be referred to the Committee on the Course and the Statutes to consider and report upon the propriety of establishing in the College a department of the Philosophy of Charity and Correction.

1877. Feb. 5. Resolution on increasing number of hours in daily course. *Resolved,* That it be referred to the Committee on the Course and the Statutes to consider and report upon the propriety of and the plan for increasing the number of hours in the daily course of the College.

1877, Feb. 5. Resolution on Department of Oriental Languages. *Resolved,* That it be referred to the Committee on the Course and the Statutes to consider and report upon the propriety of establishing in the College a department of Oriental Languages.

1877, June 4. Prize Scholarship referred to Committee on Course and Statutes. *Resolved,* That it be referred to the Committee on the Course and the Statutes to inquire into the practical operation of the system of prize scholarships established in the College by resolutions of April 3, 1871, and to report hereafter whether the said system ought to be in any manner modified or should be abolished.

1878, May 6. Resolutions on Qualifications of Candidates for admission to the College referred to Committee on Course and Statutes. *Resolved,* That it be referred to the Committee on the Course and the Statutes to inquire whether it is practicable to devise any expedient for satisfactorily ascertaining the qualifications of candidates for admission to the College, by means of which the laboriousness and duration of the stated entrance examinations may be diminished.

1878, May 6.

Resolved, That the same Committee be requested to inquire as to the advisability of allowing candidates for admission to come up for partial examination at stated periods in the years preceding their final application for admission.

1878. May 6. Resolution as to expediency of Examination of Schools by Committees of the Faculty referred to Committee on Course and Statutes.

Resolved, That the same Committee be requested to inquire further as to the expediency of instituting a system of examination, by committees of the Faculty, of such schools, in New York and elsewhere, as may desire such examination, with a view, by the publication of the results so obtained, of making known the merits of such school and of stimulating the improvement of school education in the country.

1878, May 6.

Resolved, That the Committee be requested to present their report on the subjects embraced in the foregoing resolutions on or before the first Monday in January, 1879.

1879, May 5. Volunteer Classes in Greek.

Resolved, That the Trustees have received with satisfaction the statements which have been presented to them in regard to the efforts made by Mr. A. C. Merriam, Tutor in Greek in the College, to promote facility among the students of the College in reading Greek by the formation of volunteer classes to read Greek authors at sight, and they desire to express their high appreciation of the zeal thus displayed by him in the cause of good learning, and of his earnest devotedness to his work in the College.

Resolved, That Mr. Merriam be requested to report to the President the names of the most distinguished of the students in the volunteer classes now under his instruction, and that these names, or so many of them as the President may see fit to select, be publicly announced on commencement day.

1879, June 2. Instructor in Anglo Saxon. His salary and duties.

Resolved, That there be, and hereby is, appointed an instructor in the Anglo-Saxon language, to be compensated at a rate not exceeding fifteen hundred dollars per annum, and that it be referred to the Faculty to assign such duties to such officer as may be expedient or practicable in the undergraduate course, or in such post-graduate course as in their opinion may be conducive to the advancement of learning ; also,

Resolved, That the instructor so appointed be required to assist in the examination and criticism of the English compositions of the undergraduate students, to such extent as, in the judgment of the President, may be necessary.

1879, June 2.
C. P. G. Scott
nominated In-
structor. Mr. Charles P. G. Scott was nominated for said instructorship.

INSTRUCTION IN MUSIC.

1877, Feb. 5.
Resolution on
Association for
Cultivation of
Sacred Music re-
ferred to Stand-
ing Committee. *Resolved,* That in case of the formation among the undergraduate students in Columbia College of an association for the cultivation of sacred music, with a view to the improvement of the singing in the chapel, the President be authorized to employ a competent instructor to give lessons in vocal music to the members of such association, at an expense not to exceed five dollars per week during the academic year.

1877. Nov. 5.
President to hire
piano. *Resolved,* That the President be authorized to hire a piano for the use of the College Choir in their practice, at the rate not exceeding ten dollars per month, from the present time until the first of June, 1878.

1878. Oct. 7.
President autho-
rized to employ
Dr. Pearce at $5
per week. *Resolved,* That the President be authorized to employ Dr. Pearce, instructor in vocal music, from the beginning of the first to the end of the second term in each academic year, or during the pleasure of the Trustees, at an expense not to exceed five dollars per week.

1879, May 5.
Provision for
Choir in Chapel. *Resolved,* That it be referred to the Committee on the Course and the Statutes to consider and report whether any additional provision, and if so what provision, is necessary to maintain the efficiency of the Choir in the chapel service.

1879, June 2.
Vocal Music.
Dr. Walter to
give instruction
to Chapel Choir. *Resolved,* That the President be authorized to make arrangements with Dr. Walter, Organist of the College, to give lessons in vocal music, not less frequently than once a week during the ensuing year, to members of the chapel choir, at a compensation of one hundred and fifty dollars for the entire year, to be paid in equal instalments with his salary as organist.

INVENTORY OF MOVABLE PROPERTY.

1877, Nov. 5.
President to employ experts to catalogue and value personal property.

Resolved, That the President be authorized to employ experts to catalogue and value the personal property in the School of Mines and the College to the extent that may be authorized by the Standing Committee from time to time.

LAW SCHOOL, BUILDING.

1878. Jan. 7.
Resolution on Hire of Building for Law School.

Resolved, That the Treasurer have power to hire from W. C. Schermerhorn, Esq., the building now occupied for the Law School for the term of five years from the first day of May, 1878, at the usual rent for the first three years of forty-five hundred dollars ($4,500), and for the last two years of five thousand dollars ($5,000), with a right on the part of the College to terminate the lease on any first day of May after the commencement of the term by giving to the lessor within notice of the intention to terminate it on or before the first of January next preceding such first day of May. The College to pay the Croton water rates—and with such other stipulations as may be approved by the Law Committee. Also,

Resolved, That the Clerk be authorized to sign and affix the seal to a lease of the said premises when so approved.

LAW SCHOOL, DEGREES AND EXAMINATIONS.

1874, June 1,
Law Committee to inquire as to Examinations and Degrees.

Resolved, That the Law Committee be instructed to consider the propriety of requiring a preliminary examination of applicants for admission to the School of Law who are not college graduates; also of conferring the degree of Bachelor of Laws only on such students as are college graduates or shall have attended the School of Law for three years.

1871, Dec. 7. Resolutions of Committee on School of Law as to admission, etc. *Resolved,* That the admission of students to the Law School on and after the first Wednesday in October, 1876, shall be regulated as follows :

All graduates of literary colleges will be admitted without examination. Other candidates for admission must be at least eighteen years of age and have received a good academic education, including such a knowledge of the Latin Language as is required for admission to the Freshman Class of this College.

1875, Feb. 1. Resolution on Examination for Law School lost. *Resolved,* That the examination of applicants for admission to the Law School in the Latin Language, under the terms of the resolution heretofore passed by this Board, be held upon six books of Virgil and six orations of Cicero.

1876, Feb. 7. W. H. Leggett, R. S. Bacon, D. S. Everson, Examiners. *Resolved,* That Messrs. William H. Leggett, Richard S. Bacon, and Duane S. Everson, be appointed examiners to conduct the examination of candidates for admission, and that they be paid a compensation of $50 each for their services.

1876, Feb. 7. Days for Examination for Admission to be determined. *Resolved,* That the days for holding the examinations for admission to the Law School at the beginning of the next term may be determined by agreement between Professor Dwight and the examiners, and that the Warden shall have the power of substituting other examiners in .case of the inability of any of the examiners to attend.

1876, Feb. 7. Warden to request Bar Association to appoint committee. *Resolved,* That it shall be the duty of the Warden of the Law School, prior to each concluding examination, to request the Association of the Bar of the City of New York to appoint a committee to attend such examination.

1877, June 4. Number of Examiners for admission to Law School. *Resolved,* That hereafter the Committee on the School of Law shall have power to appoint three examiners to conduct the next succeeding examination of candidates for admission to the Law School.

LAW SCHOOL, FACULTY.

1878, April 1. Resolutions respecting professorships in the Law School. *Resolved,* That all existing Professorships in the Law School are abolished : this resolution to take effect on the 15th of August, 1878.

Resolved, That on and after the 15th of August, 1878,

there shall be the following Professorships in the Law School.:

1. A Professorship of the Law of Contracts, Maritime and Admiralty Law.

There shall be assigned to this department courses of lectures on the subject of General Jurisprudence.

2. A Professorship of Real Estate and Equity Jurisprudence.

3. A Professorship of Criminal Law, Torts, and Procedure.

4. A Professorship of Constitutional History, and International and Constitutional Law and Political Science.

5. A Professorship of Medical Jurisprudence.

LAW SCHOOL, GRADUATION HONORS.

1878, April 1
Degree of LL.B
cum laude.

Resolved, 1. That students hereafter admitted, and who shall add to the study of Municipal Law the courses of instruction and recitation upon Constitutional History and Constitutional Law, Diplomatic History and International Law, and shall pass approved examinations therein, shall receive the Degree of Bachelor of Laws, "*cum laude.*" The same rule shall be extended to those hereafter admitted to whom prizes in either department shall be awarded, or of whom honorable mention shall be made by the Committee of Award.

Resolved, 2. That in the publication of the names of the graduates in the catalogue, respect shall be had to this gradation of the degree.

LAW SCHOOL, INSTRUCTION.

1874, Dec. 7.
Degree of Master of Laws.

Resolved, That a course of study shall be organized in the Law School embracing instruction in Political Science, International, Constitutional, and Admiralty law, and upon special topics of Municipal Law to be hereafter assigned, such course to occupy a Third Year.

The Degree of Master of Laws shall be conferred on such graduates of the Law School attending this course as shall pass a satisfactory examination.

It may also be conferred on like terms on graduates of other Law Schools who have pursued, before their entrance into this Institution, a course of study equivalent to that prescribed by this resolution.

1876, May 1.
Resolution to refer to Board of College and Warden of Law School to report scheme.

Resolved, That it be referred to the Board of the College and Warden of the Law School to report a scheme for the duties of the Professor of History, Political Science, and International Law.

1878, April 1.
Warden to assign duties to any professor.

Resolved, That the Warden shall have power temporarily to assign any Professor to special duties not within the strict range of his professorship, including the duty to act as Secretary of the Faculty, and keep the minutes of proceedings. He shall also, from time to time, assign to one or more of the Professors the duty of preparing Moot Court cases for argument, or presiding at the Moot Courts, and instructing students in the mode of preparing causes for argument.

LAW SCHOOL, REGISTRAR.

1878, April 1.
Registrar of Law School.

Resolved, That an officer, to be styled the Registrar of the Law School, shall be appointed by the Committee on the School of Law on the nomination of the Warden ; and it shall be his duty, under the direction of the Warden, to keep the Law School office open, keep the books, address catalogues, and do such other matters of detail as may be assigned to him by the Warden ; and he shall receive an annual compensation of one thousand dollars, payable in instalments at the times at which the salaries of the officers of the College are payable, he to hold his office during the pleasure of the Trustees or of the Committee.

LAW SCHOOL, SUPPORT OF.

Resolved, That, with the consent of the Professor of Municipal Law, the regulations for the support of the Law School, adopted by the Board of Trustees on the first day of February, 1864, are repealed, such repeal to take effect on the 1st of October, 1878.

Resolved, That on and after the 1st of October, 1878, the regulations for the support of the Law School shall be as follows :

1. The tuition fees shall be one hundred dollars per year.

2. The fees shall not be remitted unless by order of the Trustees.

3. The fees shall be collected by the Warden of the School, and be, from time to time, as received, paid by him to the Treasurer.

4. All the expenses of the School will be paid by the Trustees.

Resolved, That the following shall be the regulations under which appropriations shall be made and expended for the maintenance of the Law School :

1. On estimates presented by the Warden, the Trustees will, in each year, make appropriations for the next succeeding year for commencement, for the separate annual catalogue of the School, for printing, for advertising, for supplies, and for the Library.

2. All such appropriations shall be expended under the direction of the Warden ; and any extraordinary appropriation of any kind, not included in the above classification, shall be expended under the like direction, unless otherwise ordered.

3. No bill for the expenditures authorized by any appropriation above directed to be expended under the direction of the Warden shall be paid, unless it shall be approved and certified by the Warden.

LEASES AND RENTS.

1874, Feb. 2.
Application of
Alvin Higgins.

Mr. Nash presented a communication from Mr. S. F. Cowdrey, on behalf of Mr. Alvin Higgins, asking for relief from the action of the Standing Committee, in granting a lease of lot 179, in Barclay street, to Mr. Welsh, and presented the following resolution, which was lost:

1874, Feb. 2.
Mr. Nash's reso-
lution lost.

"*Resolved,* That the matter of the lease of lot No. 179, in Barclay street, be recommitted to the Standing Committee, with the recommendation that such lease be given to the holder of the present term, Mr. Alvin Higgins, provided he shall accept such lease upon the same terms as shall be required of any other proposed lessee."

1874, Nov. 2.
Standing Com-
mittee to grant
leases, etc.

Resolved, That the Standing Committee have power to grant renewal or original leases of the lots hereinafter enumerated, upon such terms as it shall deem expedient, that is to say, of lots 48, 50, 52, 54, 56, 58, 60, and 62, in Murray street, the present leases of which will expire on the first day of May next.

1875, Oct. 4,
Standing Com-
mittee to grant
leases.

Resolved, That the Standing Committee have power to grant leases, upon such terms as it shall judge to be expedient, of the lots known by the map numbers, 201 in Barclay street, 204 and 204A in Barclay street and Park place, and 211 in Barclay street, the present leases of which will expire respectively on the first day of February, the first day of March, and the first day of May next.

1876, Oct. 2.
Clerk to affix
seal.

Resolved, That the Clerk be authorized to sign and affix the corporate seal to any proper and usual instruments in writing, on behalf of this corporation, acknowledging the receipt of such award or awards, and releasing to the Corporation of the City of New York the lands taken for such improvement.

1876. June 5.
Standing Com-
mittee to accept
surrender of
leases, etc.

Resolved, That the Standing Committee have power to accept a surrender of two leases, the one thereof of lot 200 in Barclay street, and lots 200A and 201A in Park place, and the other of lot 201 in Barclay street, and to grant in place thereof two new leases, one of the lots 200 and 200A, and the other of the lots 201 and 201A, upon such terms as the Committee shall deem to be equitable.

1876, June 5. Clerk to affix seal. *Resolved,* That the Clerk be authorized to execute and affix the seal of the College to any leases that may be granted by such Committee under the last preceding resolution.

1877. May 7. Standing Committee to accept surrender of leases, etc., in Barclay st. and Park Place. *Resolved,* That power be given to the Standing Committee to accept a surrender of two leases, the one thereof of lot 200 in Barclay street and lots 200A and 201A in Park place, and the other of lot 201 in Barclay street, and to grant in place thereof new leases, comprising together the same lots, upon such terms as the Committee shall deem to be equitable, and that the Clerk be authorized to execute and affix the seal to such leases.

1878, Nov. 4. Resolution authorizing Standing Committee to accept surrender of lease, 211 Barclay. *Resolved,* That, if the Standing Committee shall deem it to be for the interest of the College, they be authorized to direct the acceptance of a surrender of the lease of the lot of land known on the College map by the number 211 in Barclay street, upon such terms as they shall judge to be expedient.

1879, Jan. 6. Standing Committee to grant renewal leases on lots II. & III. in Park Place, and an original lease of 211 Barclay street. *Resolved,* That the Standing Committee have power to grant renewal leases, in the usual form, of the lots known on the College map by the numbers II. and III. in Park place, and also an original lease, upon such terms as the Committee shall deem for the interest of the College, of the lot known on the same map by the number 211 in Barclay street, to which leases the corporate seal shall be affixed.

1879, Feb. 3. Standing Committee to report on expediency of reducing rents. *Resolved,* That it be referred to the Standing Committee to consider and report whether it is expedient to make any, and if any what, reductions in the rents reserved by leases of any of the lots of the lower estate.

1879, Mar. 3. Clerk to sign and affix seal to a re-extension of lease, D. E. Valkenburgh. *Resolved,* That the Clerk be authorized to sign and affix the corporate seal to a re-extension of the lease, bearing date the first day of February, 1864, made to Daniel E. Valkenburgh, of the lot designated as lot C in the Fifth avenue, it being alleged that such lease is lost.

1879, Mar. 3. Rents of certain lots to be permanently reduced. *Resolved,* That the rents of the following lots be permanently reduced :

Of lot 48, in Murray street, to $1,400.
" 50, " " " $1,400.
" II., in Park place, to $1,500.
" III., " " $1,500.

And that the leases of lots 48 and 50 Murray street be modified accordingly by an instrument in writing, to which the seal of the College shall be affixed.

LEAVE OF ABSENCE.

1875, Oct. 4.
Leave of absence to H. Newton.

Resolved, That leave of absence, without pay, be granted to Henry Newton, Assistant in Geology in the School of Mines, until the first day of January, 1876, and that the Professor be authorized to appoint, with the approval of the President, some suitable person to discharge the duties of Assistant during such absence, to be paid at the same rate as the regular Assistant.

1878, Jan. 7.
Leave of absence to Prof. Peck.

Resolved, That leave of absence be granted to Professor Peck for the remainder of this academic year, or for such less time as the state of his health may require, and that during his absence the instruction of his classes in Mechanics and Astronomy in the College and School of Mines be assigned to his assistant, Mr. Ingersoll, and the instruction of the Senior Class in Calculus and the Sophomore Class in Surveying be assigned to Professor Van Amringe, who volunteers to take these duties without compensation.

1878. Jan. 7.
Increased pay allowed Mr. Ingersoll.

Resolved, That, in consideration of the increased duty assigned to Mr. Ingersoll, compensation be allowed him at the rate of one hundred dollars per month, so long as he shall continue to perform such duties, in addition to the compensation to which he is regularly entitled as assistant.

LIBRARIES.

1874, Mar. 2.
Beardsley's Life of Johnson.

Resolved, That fifty copies of Dr. Beardsley's Life of President Johnson be purchased by the College and distributed by the President among such libraries as he may think fit.

1874, April 6.
Journals of New York Convention given to the diocese of Albany.

Resolved, That a duplicate set of the Journals of the Convention of New York, now in the Library, be given to the Diocese of Albany.

1874, May 4. Catalogues to be printed.	*Resolved,* That the catalogue of the books, etc., in the Library be printed under the direction of the Library Committee at an expense not to exceed two thousand dollars.
1874, May 4. Catalogue of the Library to be sold.	*Resolved,* That the Catalogues of the Library, when printed, shall be sold under the direction of the Library Committee, and the proceeds paid into the Treasury.
1874, Nov. 2. Library Catalogue.	*Resolved,* That the Librarian be authorized to furnish copies of the Catalogue of the Library to the President and Professors of the College and of the School of Mines and of the School of Law, and to such public libraries as have furnished us with copies of their own catalogues.
1874, Nov. 2. 25 copies at disposal of Library Committee.	*Resolved,* Further, that twenty-five copies of the same be placed at the disposal of the Library Committee for distribution in such manner as may seem to them judicious.
1874, Dec. 7. Request of Library Committee referred to Sub-Committee on Site with power.	*Resolved,* That the Trustees be requested to appropriate to the use of the Library for the deposit of duplicates and public documents any unoccupied room in the College.
1875, Jan. 4. Invitation to A. R. Thompson.	*Resolved,* That the Trustees extend a cordial invitation to Mr. A. R. Thompson, of this city, whose donations to the Library of the College have been recently acknowledged, to visit the College and the School of Mines, and to be present at the exercises whenever it may be agreeable to him.
1875, Mar. 1. 25 additional copies of Catalogue of Library at disposal of Library Committee.	*Resolved,* That the Trustees place twenty-five additional copies of the Catalogue of the Library at the disposal of the Library Committee.
1875, May 3. Resolution to pay Librarian $300 on account of Catalogue.	*Resolved,* That the sum of three hundred dollars be paid to Mr. Betts, the Librarian, for the extra labor expended by him in the preparation of an alphabetical catalogue of the Library and conducting its publication.
1875, May 3. Resolutions to print Librarian's report and additions to Library.	*Resolved,* That the Library Committee be authorized to print in pamphlet form the Librarian's Report for the current year, with a list of additions made during that time to the Library, the cost to be defrayed from the balance of the fund heretofore appropriated for printing the catalogue.
1875, June 7. Library Committee to dispose of Catalogue.	*Resolved,* That the Library Committee be authorized to dispose of the unsold copies of the catalogue of the Library in such manner as shall be in their judgment most conducive to the interest of the College.

1876, Jan. 3.
Resolution on
Libraries refer-
red to Library
Committee.

Resolved, That it be referred to the Committee on the Library to consider and report whether it is practicable and expedient to unite the libraries of the College and of the School of Mines and the Botanical Library, so as to bring them all under the supervision of one librarian, with such assistance as he may require ; and also to report a scheme for the regulation of the united libraries such that they may be kept open and accessible to students and others, daily, and within all reasonable hours.

1876, Mar. 6.
Report of Libra-
ry Committee
on Union of Li-
braries.

Resolved, That while in the opinion of the Committee the union of the libraries of the College and of the School of Mines would be attended with some important advantages, it does not appear to them practicable to effect such union without the erection of a new building, or an enlargement of the present buildings, at an expense too great to be judiciously incurred for the purpose.

1876, Jan. 3.
Assistant to Li-
brarian and Re-
gistrar School of
Mines.

Resolved, That an assistant to the Registrar and Librarian of the School of Mines be appointed at a compensation of five hundred dollars per annum from October 1, 1875, to October 1, 1876.

1876, June 5.
Libraries of the
Literary Soci-
eties.

Resolved, That it be referred to the Standing Committee to inquire whether it is possible to make any provision for the accommodation of the Libraries of the Philolexian and Peithologian Societies, so that they can be made accessible to the members, with power to act in the case as may seem to them advisable.

1877, Oct. 1.
Librarian and
Registrar of
School of Mines
to be Librarian
only, and Regis-
trar transferred
to Dean.

Resolved, That the Librarian and Registrar of the School of Mines be hereafter charged only with the duties which properly belong to the office of Librarian, and be styled the Librarian ; also, that the duties heretofore performed by the Librarian as Registrar be transferred to the Dean of the Faculty of the School, and that, to aid him in the performance of these duties, he shall be entitled to the services of the assistant heretofore appointed to aid the Librarian and Registrar in the performance of the same duties.

1878, Mar. 4.
$6,000 appropri-
ated to Library
of Law School.

Resolved, That six thousand dollars ($6,000) be appropriated for the enlargement of the Law School Library, to be apportioned, four thousand dollars ($4,000) for the purchase of books on municipal law, and two thousand dollars ($2,000) for the purchase of books on the subject of political science, the purchase to be made under the direction of the Warden.

1878. Mar. 4.
Use of Library
School of Mines. *Resolved,* That the students of the College shall be allowed to have access to the Library of the School of Mines, and be permitted to take books therefrom, in accordance with such regulations as may be duly established by the Board of Trustees or its Library Committee.

1878, June 3.
Resolution on
access to Library of School of
Mines to professors referred to
Committee on
Library. *Resolved,* That the privilege of access to the Library of the School of Mines be granted to the Professors of said School during the absence of the Librarian, to consult but not to take out books and journals.

1878, April 1.
Librarian for
Law School. *Resolved,* That there shall be a Librarian appointed by the Committee on the School of Law on the recommendation of the Warden, whose salary shall be at the rate of five hundred dollars per annum, payable in instalments at the times at which the salaries of the officers are payable, he to hold his office during the pleasure of the Trustees on the Committee.

1879, Feb. 3.
Reference to
Committee on
Course and Statutes, and Committee on
School of Law,
as to Superintendence of the
Libraries of the
College. *Resolved,* That it be referred to the Committee on the Course and Statutes and the Committee on the School of Law to consider the necessity and expediency of the enactment of provisions to give the Committee on the Library superintendence and direction of the Libraries of all departments of the College.

LOSS OF COAT.

The President read a letter from Mr. C. D. Brower relative to a coat which had been stolen from the cloak room, upon which it was

1876, June 5.
On loss of Coat. *Resolved,* That the communication of Mr. C. D. Brower be referred to the Standing Committee, with authority to take such action on it as may seem to them just ; and that they also be authorized to consider and act upon the claim of Mr. B. F. Mayer for a similar loss, in case Mr. Mayer should lay such claim before them.

OBSERVATORY.

1874, May 4.
Astronomical
Clock. The resolution to appropriate a sum, not exceeding five hundred dollars, for the purchase of a clock for the Astronomical Observatory, was, upon the recommendation of the Standing Committee, passed for the second time.

1874, Dec. 7.
Chronometer for
Prof. Peck.

Resolved, That, in accordance with the request of Professor Peck, the sum of five hundred dollars, appropriated on the fourth day of May, 1874, for the purchase of a clock for the Astronomical Observatory, may be applied, so far as is needful, for the purchase of a break circuit chronometer.

1876, Jan. 3.
On furnishing
exact mean so-
lar time, etc.

Resolved, That, in case a proposition should be made by citizens of New York to Professor Peck to furnish by himself or his assistant, from the Observatory of the College, exact mean solar time, the Trustees are willing that engagements for that purpose be entered into, provided they impose no expense upon the College, and do not interfere with the proper duties of the Professor or his assistant, or with the uses of the Observatory for the instruction of the students.

OPTIONAL STUDIES.

1870, May 2.
Inquiry as to ex-
pediency of al-
lowing Optional
Studies.

Resolved, That it be referred to the Committee on the Statutes to inquire whether it may not be expedient and practicable so to modify the system of instruction in the College as so allow to the students of the Junior and Senior Classes some larger latitude of choice in regard to the studies pursued by them during the last two years of the course, and, in case of an affirmative decision, to report to the Trustees a scheme of instruction by which that object may be accomplished.

1870, Oct. 3.
Arrangements
for Optional
Studies of
Senior Class.

Resolved, That, in case it should appear advantageous in the preparation of optional study for the Senior Class to modify in some measure the distribution of time between the several departments of instruction, the Board of the College be authorized to make such modification; no scheme, however, to be adopted, except provisionally, until after being submitted to the Trustees and approved by them.

Resolved, That if there should appear to be serious difficulty in preparing a scheme of optional study as above, without inconveniently deranging the course of study in the lower classes and in the School of Mines, the Board of the College be authorized to adhere for the present session to the scheme of Senior studies heretofore in operation, and that they prepare and submit to the Trustees, as early as practicable, a scheme for use in future years which shall be in conformity with the resolution of the Committee on the Statutes heretofore communicated to them.

1877, Oct. 1. Addition to Optional Studies. *Resolved,* That to the optional studies, Latin and Physics, between which the members of the Senior Class are at present allowed to choose for two hours of each week, there be added, as a third, Political Economy, so that the option may be between Political Economy, Latin, and Physics.

1877, Oct. 1. Chemistry as an Optional Study. *Resolved,* That the option heretofore allowed to the students of the Senior Class between Philosophy and Chemistry, which was discontinued during the last academic year in consequence of the absence of the Professor of Chemistry, be now once more allowed, the students preferring Chemistry to attend with the Class in Theoretic Chemistry in the School of Mines three hours per week.

PRINTING.

1874, Feb. 2. Statutes to be Printed. *Resolved,* That an edition of five hundred copies of the Statutes of the College be printed with the usual accompanying matter for the use of the College; also, that one hundred copies of the resolutions of the Board of Trustees, passed since the spring of 1868, be printed for the use of the Trustees.

1874, Feb. 2. Dr. Haight's Address to be Printed. *Resolved,* That one thousand copies of the address of the Rev. Dr. Haight on the life of the late President Nathaniel F. Moore, delivered in the College chapel, be printed at the expense of the Trustees.

1874, May 4. Catalogue of Library to be Printed. *Resolved,* That the catalogue of the books, etc., in the Library be printed under the direction of the Library Committee, at an expense not to exceed two thousand dollars.

1875, April 5. President to print Resolutions on Expenditures. *Resolved,* That the President shall have the resolutions on general expenditures printed and distributed to each of the Professors.

1875, May 3. Resolution referred to Special Committee to Reduce the Cost of Printing. *Resolved,* That it be referred to a special committee of three to consider and report upon the expediency of reducing the cost of printing and advertising, both of the College and School of Mines, and to report any regulations upon the subject, but more especially upon the printing, publication, and distribution of the annual catalogue.

1875, May 3.
Resolution to print 500 copies Catalogue School of Mines Library.

Resolved, That five hundred (500) copies of a catalogue of the Library of the School of Mines be printed at a cost not to exceed eight hundred dollars ($800).

1875, Oct. 4.
Resolutions on Printing and Advertising.

Resolved, 1. That the appropriation for printing catalogues for the present year shall be $1,750.

Resolved, 2. That the appropriation for general printing and advertising shall be $1,500.

Resolved, 3. That advertisements of the College and School of Mines for the present year shall not be extended beyond the following journals published in the city of New York, and representing the various political parties and Christian denominations :

Times, Tribune, World, Herald, Express, Evening Post, Commercial Advertiser, Nation, Church Journal, Christian Intelligencer, Observer, Evangelist, Examiner and Chronicle, Christian Advocate, and the journals which may be edited and published by the undergraduates of the College and the School of Mines.

Resolved, 4. That the catalogues shall be prepared and edited by the Secretary of the Faculty of the College, and that all the printing and advertising of the College and School of Mines shall be given out through and be superintended by him, as may be directed by the Trustees, the President, or Faculty, and that two hundred and fifty dollars a year be allowed to the Secretary of the Faculty for his preparation of said catalogue and supervision of said printing and advertising.

1875, Nov. 1.
Resolution of Faculty to authorize Printing, etc., General Catalogue referred to Standing Committee.

Resolved, That the Trustees be respectfully requested to authorize the preparation and printing during the current academic year of the general catalogue of the officers, alumni, and students of the College, the same to be complete at the next annual commencement, and to embrace the record to the close of the second triennium, since the publication of the last general catalogue, and to the close of the Centennial Year of the Republic.

1875, Nov. 1.
General Catalogue to be Published.

Resolved, That the catalogue of the governors, trustees, and officers, and of the alumni and other graduates of the College, including those graduating in 1876, be published after the next annual commencement.

1875, Nov. 1. Resolutions on Printing and Advertising. *Resolved,* That the appropriation made October 4, 1875, of $1,750, for printing catalogues for the present year, and $1,500, for general printing and advertising, be appropriated as follows :

For catalogues of the College, including in one volume the catalogues of the College, the Law School, the School of Mines, and Medical School, and also including the separate catalogue of the College, $1,100.

For separate catalogue of School of Mines, $650.

Printing and advertising of College, $750.

For printing and advertising of School of Mines, $750.

1876, June 5. Resolution on Publishing Advertisements. *Resolved,* That for the next year, and for every year thereafter, until the further order of the Trustees, advertisements for the College shall be published only in the following journals published in the city of New York :

The *Times, Tribune, World, Evening Post,* and the journals which may be edited and published by the undergraduates of the College and School of Mines, and advertisements for the School of Mines may be published in the same papers, and the *Herald, Commercial Advertiser, Nation, Church Journal, Christian Intelligencer, Evangelist, Examiner and Chronicle,* and *Christian Advocate,* and in no other journals or newspapers.

1877, May 7. Printing Roman Antiquities. *Resolved,* That an appropriation of $72 be made for printing 500 copies of questions in Roman Antiquities for and under the direction of Professor Schmidt.

1878, May 6. Handbook, etc. to be stereotyped and distributed annually. *Resolved,* That a handbook of information, containing the names of the officers, and such information as the President may think it expedient to insert in regard to the existing regulations, the course of instruction, the facilities for instruction, and other matters tending to display the advantages presented to students, shall be stereotyped and issued annually to students, and otherwise distributed as the President may deem advisable.

1879, Feb. 3. Standing Committee to Order and Pay Bills for Handbook. *Resolved,* That bills for stereotype plates for and printing the handbook of the College be referred to the Standing Committee, with power to order their payment, and that the sum necessary therefor be and is hereby appropriated.

PRIZES.

1874, May 4.
Greek Prizes.
Resolved, That the resolutions of the Trustees, establishing junior prizes in Greek, and prescribing as a condition that the competitors for such prizes shall not have appeared in any term or examination record deficient in scholarship in any department for the two years next preceding, be amended by striking out the words, "shall not have appeared deficient in scholarship in any department," etc., and inserting the words, "shall be in good and regular standing in their class."

1875, Dec. 6.
Resolutions of
Mr. Ruggles on
Prizes, $150, in
Political Science
Resolved, That he is informed by the Warden of the Law School that one of the graduates of the School, being desirous of founding one or two prizes, not exceeding in the aggregate one hundred and fifty dollars yearly, proposed to pay that sum at once for the first year, that it may be paid to the most deserving scholars in the course of lectures on Political Science to be delivered this year by Mr. Burgess, as authorized by the Law School Committee.

Resolved, That the Warden of the Law School be authorized to pay such sum out of such donation, and that the same be duly notified to the class in due time before the commencement of the course.

1879, Jan. 3.
Bequest of J.
Winthrop Chandler of $1,000 Income to be given
to Author of
Best Essay on
History of Civil
Government in
America, or
other Historical
Subject, etc.
A communication was received from the executors of J. Winthrop Chanler, deceased, informing the Trustees of a bequest made by his will in the words next following, that is to say :

". . . To the Trustees of Columbia College in the city of New York, the sum of one thousand dollars, to be invested, and kept invested, and the income thereof to be given annually, on the commencement day, to the undergraduate member of the Senior Class of said College who shall be the author of the best original manuscript essay in English prose on the history of civil government in America, or some other historical subject, the same to be determined by the judgment and decision of the Faculty of said College."

PROFESSORSHIPS AND PROFESSORS.

1874. Feb. 2. Assistant in Metallurgy referred

Resolved, That there be appointed an assistant in Metallurgy in the School of Mines, to be paid at the rate of one thousand dollars per annum, payments to be made in equal instalments at the times already fixed for payment of the assistants now employed in said School.

Referred to Standing Committee, reported unfavorably, and lost.

1875, May 3, Resolution to Appoint Assistant in Department of Physics referred to Standing Committee.

Resolved, That there be appointed an assistant in the department of Physics in the College, at an annual salary of one thousand dollars, to be paid in four equal instalments on the usual College quarter days, this resolution to take effect from the first day of October next.

1876, April 3, Resolution on Chair of History, Political Science, etc.

Resolved, That the College hereby establishes a Professorship of History, Political Science, and International Law, the duties of which shall be divided between the College and the Law School, in such manner and proportion as the Committee on the Course and the Law School Committee shall deem advisable, or as may be hereafter prescribed by order of this Board.

1876, Dec. 4. Second Assistant in Assaying.

Resolved, That a second assistant in Assaying be appointed at a salary of $500 per annum, to be paid in equal instalments at the times at which the assistants already in the School are paid.

1877, Feb. 5. Resolution on Adjunct Professor Moral and Intellectual Philosophy.

Resolved, That there be appointed an Adjunct Professor of Moral and Intellectual Philosophy, whose duty it shall be to give a course of instruction in the College in the principles of philosophy and psychology, with special reference to the results of modern biological research as affecting these sciences.

1877, Feb. 5. To hold office Three Years, or during pleasure, etc.

Resolved, That, in pursuance of the preceding resolution, the Board now proceed to appoint an Adjunct Professor, to hold office for the period of three years from the time of entering upon his duties, or during the pleasure of this Board, and to receive a salary at the rate of twenty-five hundred dollars ($2,500) per annum.

1877, April 2.
Reorganization
of the School of
Mines.
1. As to Chem-
istry.
Resolved, That the chair of Chemistry in the College, and also the chair of Analytical and Applied Chemistry in the School of Mines, be and the same are hereby abolished, and that there be established instead thereof a chair, to be entitled the chair of Chemistry, to be charged with the duty of giving instruction in all the branches of chemical science required to be taught either in the College or in the said School of Mines, except in Blowpipe Analysis, which, till further order, shall continue to be taught as at present.

Resolved, That the Professor of Chemistry shall personally give instruction to all the classes in general chemistry, both elementary and theoretical, and in the applications of chemistry to the arts, and shall supervise and direct the instruction in assaying and in all branches of chemical analysis (except for the present blowpipe analysis), daily visiting the laboratories for that purpose ; that he shall be aided in these last-named branches by three principal assistants, to be styled Instructors, who shall be severally charged with the immediate duty of instruction in Quantitative Analysis, Qualitative Analysis, and Assaying, both in the lecture room and in the laboratories, and shall always, during the hours assigned to the students for their practical work, be personally present in such laboratories, conferring with and aiding every student at his working table ; and that further to aid the students in their laboratory practice, there shall be appointed a second assistant for each of the said laboratories ; also, that to aid the Professor in his lecture room instruction, there be appointed an assistant holding the place of the present assistant in General Chemistry.

Resolved, That the Professor of Chemistry shall be compensated for his services at the rate of $7,500 per annum ; the three principal assistants at the rate of $2,000 per annum each ; the three second assistants at the rate of $500 per annum each ; and the lecture room assistant at the rate of $1,000 per annum.

Resolved, That these resolutions shall take effect from and after the 15th day of August, 1877, and that on Monday the seventh day of May now next ensuing, this Board will proceed to the election of a Professor of Chemistry, and of his several assistants.

Resolved, That instruction in elementary chemistry shall be given to the Sophomore Class in College one hour per week throughout the year, and that to this extent only shall chemistry form a part of the compulsory course of instruction in College ; that the hours of attendance of the Classes of the School of Mines for instruction in Chemistry shall be such as may be prescribed in the scheme of attendance ; also, that, so soon as it shall be found practicable, the undergraduate students in the College may be permitted to attend any of the above described courses of instruction in elementary, theoretic, analytic, applied, or blowpipe chemistry, as elective studies.

I.—As to Geology.

Resolved, That instruction in geology, lithology, and mineralogy shall be given to the Senior Class in College, by the present Professor of Geology and Palæontology, one hour per week throughout the year, or during one session of the year as may be hereafter determined, and that to this extent only shall those subjects form part of the compulsory course of instruction in College; but that, so soon as practicable, the undergraduate students in College may be permitted to attend the lectures of the same Professor, given in the School of Mines, in General Geology, Economic Geology, Botany, and Zoology, as elective studies.

Resolved, That, in view of the assignment to the Professor of Geology of instruction in the undergraduate course, his salary be at the rate of $7,500 per annum, to commence on the fifteenth day of August, 1877.

III.—As to Engineering.

Resolved, That the chair of Civil and Mining Engineering in the School of Mines be and the same is hereby abolished, and that there be and is hereby created instead thereof a chair, to be entitled the chair of Engineering, to be charged with the duty of giving instruction in all the branches of engineering science required to be taught in said School.

Resolved, That the Professor of Engineering shall personally give instruction in the principles of Civil, Mining, and Mechanical Engineering and Geodesy, and shall direct, and, so far as circumstances will allow, shall personally superintend the course of practical instruction in Drawing, in Geometrical, Geodetic and Topographical Surveying, and in Operative Mining; that he shall be aided in the discharge of these duties last enumerated by an assistant in Drawing, who shall be the immediate instructor in the principles and practice of Drawing, and shall be the Superintendent of the Drawing Academy; and by an Adjunct in Practical Mining and Surveying, who shall take charge of surveying parties in the field, and (during the vacation) of parties formed for practice in operative mining, and shall also give instruction in the preparation of ores for reduction.

Resolved, That the Professor of Engineering shall be compensated for his services at the rate of $7,500 per annum, his adjunct at the rate of $3,000, and his assistant in drawing at the rate of $2,000 per annum.

Resolved, That these resolutions shall take effect from and after the fifteenth day of August, 1877, and that on Monday, the seventh day of May now next ensuing, this Board will proceed to the election of a Professor of Engineering, and of his adjunct and assistant.

IV.—As to Metallurgy.

Resolved, That there be appointed a lecturer, or nonresident professor, to give instruction on the Metallurgy of Iron and Steel to students of the School of Mines, the extent of such course of instruction, and the compensation of the lecturer, to be fixed by resolution to be adopted hereafter.

1877, May 7, Resolution on Appointment of Professors.

Resolved, That hereafter all appointments of Professors shall, in the first instance, be for three years, or during the pleasure of the Trustees, and that in each case, after the expiration of such three years, or earlier vacancy of the office, the Trustees will proceed to fill the same anew, upon such terms as to tenure as shall then seem expedient under the circumstances.

1877, June 4. Term of Office of Adjunct Professor of Surveying.

Resolved, That the term of office of the Adjunct Professor of Surveying and Practical Mining shall commence on the first day of July, 1877.

1877, June 4. Supplementary Resolutions to Resolutions of April 2.

Resolved, That there be appointed an assistant to the Professor of Engineering, to be styled an Instructor in Mechanical Engineering, whose duty it shall be to give practical instruction in the management of machines and engines, and in the construction and use of tools, and also to aid in giving instruction in Surveying and in Drawing, and who shall be compensated at the rate of $2,000 per annum.

Resolved, That the style of the assistant in Drawing shall be Instructor in Drawing.

1877, June 4.
Resolution on
Appointments
of Adjuncts, etc.

Resolved, That all appointments that may be made at this meeting of adjuncts, instructors, tutors, and assistants in the College and in the School of Mines shall be for the term of one year only, or during the pleasure of this Board, and that in each case, after the expiration of such one year, or earlier vacancy of the office, the Trustees will proceed to fill the same anew, upon such terms as to tenure as shall then seem expedient under the circumstances.

1877, Oct. 1.
Resolution on
Appointment of
Assistant to
Professor Bur-
gess.

Resolved, That there be appointed an assistant to the Professor of History and Political Science, to serve for one year, at a salary of fifteen hundred dollars per annum, payable in instalments at the same time as the payments made to the other officers, whose duty it shall be to give instruction in the undergraduate department, under the direction of the Professor, in Political Economy and such other subjects connected with his department as the Professor, with the approval of the President, may see fit to assign him.

1878, April 1.
Resolutions as to
Professorships
in Law School.

Resolutions of this date provide for the reorganization of the Law School (see Law School, Faculty).

1878, May 6.
Resolution on
the use of the
Official Title of
the School of
Mines by Pro-
fessors, etc.

Resolved, That this Board deem it inexpedient and improper that any professor, adjunct professor, instructor, or assistant in the School of Mines, without the previous approval or assent of this Board, use the official title of the School or of the College, or to refer to his professional connection therewith, in any opinion or certificate which he may give as to the merits or claim, either relative or positive, of any association or company engaged in manufacturing, mining, or other practical business, or as to any scientific or practical invention.

1878, May 6.
Copy of same to
be communi-
cated to Dean
of School of
Mines and by
him to the sev-
eral Professors,
etc.

Resolved, That a copy of the foregoing resolution be certified to the Dean of the School of Mines, to be by him communicated and made known to the several professors, adjunct professors, instructors, and assistants in the School.

1878, June 3,
Adjunct Profes-
sor in History,
etc.

Resolved, That this Board establish an Adjunct Professorship in History, Political Science, and International Law, the Professor to be charged principally with the duty of giving instruction in Political Economy.

PUBLIC WORSHIP.

1876, Nov. 6.
Resolutions on
Public Worship.

Resolved, That in the judgment of this Board it is inexpedient to repeal the statute on public worship.

Resolved, That the President be directed to call the attention of the Faculty to the said statute, and to inform them that the Board requests and expects compliance with it in future by the officers of the College.

Resolved, That attendance on the chapel service be hereafter required of the tutors in the academic department, and that the statutes be enlarged so as to include them.

Resolved, That it be the duty of the President to ascertain, by public roll call in the chapel, or otherwise, what students are absent from the daily prayers.

Resolved, That if any student shall absent himself from more than one-fourth of the required chapel services during any one term, he shall cease to be a candidate for a degree.

1877, Feb. 5,
Resolution on
Appointment of
Roll   Officers,
$50 per annum.

Resolved, That compensation be allowed to the students appointed by the President to keep the roll of attendance in the chapel, one for each class, at the rate of $50 per annum, to be paid, in two equal instalments, on the first of February and the first of June, but each student appointed to keep the roll shall forfeit one dollar for each day on which he shall be absent from chapel service, unless he provide a substitute.

1879, March 3.
President to Appoint an Additional Roll Officer.

Resolved, That the President be authorized to appoint an additional roll officer in the chapel to keep the record of the attendance of the members of the choir, to be compensated at the same rate as the class roll officers now employed, such appointment only to be made in case other methods of securing regularity shall be found ineffectual.

REPAIRS AND ALTERATIONS.

1875, May 3.
Resolution referred to Standing Committee.

Resolved, That the President be and hereby is authorized to audit such bills as were incurred for repairs, alterations, furniture, and fixtures in the School of Mines previous to the resolution of April 5th, 1875, which regulates such expenditures for the future, and that the same, if further approved by the Standing Committee, be paid by the Treasurer.

1875, June 7.
President to direct small repairs.

Resolved, That the President be authorized, from time to time, to direct such small repairs to be made as ought to be promptly attended to.

1875, June 7.
Standing Committee to employ an Architect.

Resolved, That the Standing Committee have power, from time to time, to employ an architect to superintend and direct the making of any repairs or performance of any other work, in regard to which, in the judgment of the Committee, his intervention would be of advantage to the College.

1875, June 7.
Resolution referred to Standing Committee with power.

Resolved, That the Librarian be authorized, under the direction of the President, to cause the room lately appropriated in the College building for the use of the Library to be cleaned, painted, kalsomined, and furnished with shelves, in accordance with the estimates presented by the Librarian, and that a sum not exceeding one hundred dollars ($100) be appropriated for the purpose of defraying the cost of such work and of the labor necessary for removing the books.

1875, Oct. 4.
Resolution confirming action of Standing Committee.

Resolved, That this Board confirms the action of the Standing Committee in directing, in the vacation without the previous sanction of the Trustees, certain repairs to be made, appearing by the minutes of such Committee, and the necessity for which was first called to their attention after the last preceding meeting of the Trustees.

1875, Dec. 6.
President to direct small repairs, etc.

Resolved, That the authority given by resolution of this Board, adopted on the seventh day of June, 1875, to the President, to direct small repairs to be made, be extended so as to authorize him to direct small repairs to buildings, furniture, or fixtures, provided the cost of the same in any case shall not exceed the sum of twenty-five dollars ($25).

1876. June 5. Standing Committee to inquire as to Storerooms, etc., School of Mines

Resolved, That it be referred to the Standing Committee to inquire whether a due regard for the health of the assistant employed in the storeroom for the apparatus of the School of Mines requires that the apartments now used for that purpose in the basement of the chapel should be abandoned, and, if so, what other suitable accommodations can be found for storing the apparatus, with power to make such change as may seem to them advisable.

1877, June 4. Standing Committee to have power to enlarge Chapel.

Resolved, That the Standing Committee have power to enlarge the chapel, by including within it the space now occupied by the vestibule and staircase, and to make a new access to the library, with such alterations to the library room as may in that case become expedient, provided, however, that this authority shall not be exercised unless it shall appear that, owing to the increase of the number of students, an enlargement of the chapel will be necessary.

1877, Nov. 5. Request of Professor of Geology for Northeast Room in Basement, referred to Standing Committee with power.

Resolved, That the request of the Professor of Geology, that the northeast room in the basement of the School of Mines be fitted for the purposes of a conference room, be referred to the Standing Committee, with power.

1878, April 1. Resolution on Boilers in School of Mines referred to Standing Committee.

Resolved, That it be referred to the Standing Committee to make inquiry concerning the sufficiency of the boilers in the School of Mines to heat all the building during the winter, and to report what measures, if any, are necessary to make the apparatus more effective.

1879, Jan. 6. Standing Committee to make Alterations of Chapel for Sittings of 300 students, etc.

Resolved, That it be referred to the Standing Committee to make, before the next fall session, such alterations of the chapel as shall provide sittings for three hundred students, and shall allow more rapid egress than can now be had.

RESIGNATIONS.

1877, Jan. 8. On Resignation of Mr. Rutherfurd.

A communication from Mr. Rutherfurd was received and read, whereby he presented his resignation as a Trustee, for the reason that he was absent in the summers, and was prevented by ill-health from attending the meetings in the winter with any regularity.

1877, Jan. 8.
Resolution on
Resignation of
Mr. Rutherfurd.

Resolved, That, in the judgment of this Board, the counsel of Mr. Rutherfurd, as one of its members, is of such importance, though his attendance may be only occasional, that his resignation ought not to be accepted, if he will withdraw it.

Resolved, That the Clerk communicate a copy of the foregoing entry to Mr. Rutherfurd, with a request that he will withdraw his resignation.

SALARIES.

1874, Jan. 5.
$1,000 to be added to Prof. Joy's Salary.

Resolved, That after the said first day of May one thousand dollars be added to the salary of Professor Joy, in lieu of the right to occupy the house on the College green, heretofore assigned to his use and now required for academic purposes.

1875, April 5.
Salary of Mr. Waldo increased.

Resolved, That the salary of the assistant to the Professor of Mathematics and Astronomy in the Observatory be increased from six hundred dollars ($600) per annum, the amount fixed by resolution, March 31st, 1873, to one thousand dollars ($1,000) per annum, said assistant no longer to be provided with lodgings in the College building: payment of the same to be made in six equal instalments at the same times as heretofore.

Resolved, That this resolution take effect from the fifteenth day of February last, being the day on which Mr. Waldo reported for duty on his return from the "Transit of Venus expedition."

1875, Nov. 1.
Salary of Assistant Professor of Municipal Law.

Resolved, That the first instalment of the salary of the assistant Professor of Municipal Law, heretofore directed to be paid on the fifteenth day of January in each year, be hereafter payable on the fifteenth day of December.

1875, Feb. 7.
Resolutions of Committee on Salaries.

Resolved, 1. That, until the further action of this Board, the salaries of the Professors in the academic department of Greek, Chemistry, Mathematics and Astronomy, Moral and Intellectual Philosophy, Mathematics, Mechanics and Physics, and Latin, be fixed at $7,500 per annum for each.

Resolved, 2. That, until the further action of this Board, an additional allowance of $500 per annum be made to the Senior Professor who shall, during the absence or illness of the President, discharge his duties.

Resolved, 3. That, until the further action of this Board, the salary of the Gebhard Professor be fixed at $3,375 per annum, in addition to what he receives from the Gebhard fund.

Resolved, 4. That, until the further action of this Board, the salaries of the tutors in the academic department be fixed at $2,000 per annum.

Resolved, 5. That, until the further action of this Board, the salary of the Treasurer be fixed at $7,500 per annum.

Resolved, 6. That, until the further action of this Board, the salary of the Clerk of this Board be fixed at $1,200 per annum.

Resolved, 7. That the foregoing resolutions shall take effect to apply to all payments of salaries affected by them to be made after the first day of January, 1876.

1876, May 1. Resolution on Salary of Professor of History, Political Science, &c.   *Resolved*, That, during the pleasure of the Trustees, the salary of the Professor of History, Political Science, and International Law shall be seventy-five hundred dollars ($7,500), in full compensation for his services both in the College and in the School of Law, to be paid out of the general fund of the College, and to take effect on his entering upon the duties of his office.

1876, Nov. 6. Compensation to Instructors in French and German.   *Resolved*, That the compensation to be allowed to each one of the Instructors in French and German in the School of Mines be $3,300 per annum, and that the next quarterly payment be made at that rate.

SCHOLARSHIPS AND FELLOWSHIPS.

1871, April 3. Scheme of Scholarships reported by the Committee on the Statutes.   1. There shall be established for competition by members of the Freshman Class in this College, two scholarships, one in Classics and one in Mathematics, of the annual value of one hundred dollars each. The subjects of examination shall be the regular studies of the class for the year.

2. There shall be established, for competition by members of the Sophomore Class, four scholarships, two in Classics and two in Mathematics, of the annual value of one hundred dollars each. For two of these scholarships, one in each department, the subjects shall be the regular studies of the class for the year; for the other two, extra studies shall be assigned by the Professors in the respective departments, with the approval of the President, at the beginning of the academic year.

3. There shall be established, for competition by members of the Junior Class, six scholarships, of the annual value of one hundred dollars each, three in literary and three in scientific studies, as follows : one in Latin, one in Logic and English Literature, one in History and Rhetoric, one in Chemistry, one in Mechanics, and one in Physics. The subjects of examination shall be the studies of the year, and additional subjects in the respective departments to be designated by the several Professors, with the approval of the President, at the beginning of the academic year.

The above scholarships shall be severally held for the term of one year, and competition for the same shall be open to the members of the respective classes who are in good and regular standing in their class.

The examinations for the several scholarships shall be held at or immediately subsequent to the final college examination. The details of time and mode of conducting the examinations shall be prescribed by the Board of the College.

1871, April 3. Scheme of Fellowships reported by the Committee on the Statutes.

There shall be established in this College two fellowships, one in Literature, the other in Science, of the annual value of five hundred dollars each ; to be held by the successful competitors for the term of three years, and to be conferred under the following conditions :

Said fellowships shall be open for competition to such students of each graduating class as shall have been members of the College for the three preceding years, and are in all respects in good and regular standing in their class.

The subjects of examination for the fellowship in Literature shall be the studies of the Senior year in Greek, Latin, and Intellectual and Moral Philosophy, with such additional reading in the several departments as may be prescribed at the beginning of the year by the Board of the College.

The subjects of examination for the fellowship in Science shall be in like manner the studies of the Senior year in Chemistry, Geology, Astronomy, Calculus, and Physics, with such additional subjects in the several departments as may be prescribed at the beginning of the year by the Board of the College.

The examinations for fellowships shall be held immediately after the final examination of the Senior Class, and shall be in writing. The mode of conducting the examinations shall be prescribed by the Board of the College, who are authorized to invite the co-operation of competent alumni. The President of the College and the Professors in whose departments the students are competing shall be present during the whole examination.

The Fellows shall continue their studies, under the direction of the President of the College, for the period of their fellowship, and shall report to him from time to time in accordance with his instructions. If any Fellow shall fail to comply with these conditions, or with any which may be enacted by the Trustees, he shall be liable to forfeit his fellowship.

1871, April 3.
Resolutions of the Board of Trustees as to the foregoing schemes. *Resolved,* That the plan reported by the Committee on the Statutes, providing for the establishment of scholarships and fellowships in the College, be adopted, and that the Board of the College be requested to make the necessary announcements and arrangements for carrying the same into effect, so that the first competitive examination for said scholarships and fellowships may be held immediately after the final examination of the classes of June, 1872.

Resolved, That the payments which may become due in each academic year, on account of the scholarships and fellowships provided for as above, shall be made in two equal instalments, payable on the fifteenth days of November and May.

1874, Nov. 2.
Fellowships referred to Board of College. *Resolved,* That it be referred to the Board of the College to consider and report whether it is expedient to make

any, and if so what, changes in the conditions upon the fulfilment of which fellowships may be held and enjoyed.

1875, Nov. 1. Division of Scholarships. *Whereas,* Certain of the scholarships awarded at the last Commencement were divided so that as to each of the scholarships so divided one-half should be paid to one student and one-half to another. Therefore,

Resolved, That as the above awards have been actually made this Board confirms them so far as to authorize the Treasurer to pay the stipends accordingly for the present year. But it is further

Resolved, That it is the judgment of this Board that under the regulations heretofore made for the establishment of scholarships and fellowships the same cannot be divided.

1877. April 2. Resolution establishing Five Free Scholarships named Schermerhorn Scholarships. *Resolved,* That on the foundation made by the will of the late John Jones Schermerhorn and the payment by his executors of five thousand dollars to the Treasurer there shall be established five free scholarships in the College to be named the Schermerhorn Scholarships, the nomination to which shall belong to the testator's nearest male relative in each generation during his lifetime.

1877, April 2. Scholarship in Chemistry for Sophomore Class. *Resolved,* That there be established for competition by members of the Sophomore Class, to be awarded in this and each succeeding year, a Scholarship in Chemistry of the value of one hundred dollars, to be subject to all the regulations in regard to scholarships. Also,

Resolved, That the Scholarship in Chemistry heretofore awarded to members of the Junior Class be abolished after the end of the present academic year.

1878, April 1. Provisions relating to fellowships repealed. *Resolved,* That in the scheme of scholarships and fellowships established by resolutions of the Trustees, adopted April 3, 1871, the provisions relating to fellowships to be conferred by competitive examination, be, and the same hereby are, repealed.

1878, April 1. Mode of conferring fellowships. *Resolved,* That in lieu of the fellowships provided for in said scheme there be established two fellowships, one in Science and one in Letters, of the annual value of five hundred dollars each, to be held severally for the term of three years, and to be conferred annually by the Trustees, on nomination by the Faculty of the College, upon such graduates as propose to enter upon a course of study for higher attainments in letters or science with no utilitarian object, and who shall be adjudged by the Faculty to be capable of attaining, and likely to attain, distinction in such course of study.

1878, April 1. Fellows to pursue a course of study, and report to President.
Resolved, That the Fellows so appointed shall pursue a course of study, under the direction of the President of the College, for the period of their fellowship, and shall report to him from time to time in accordance with his instructions; and that, if any Fellow shall fail to comply with these conditions, or with any other which may be enacted by the Trustees, he shall be liable to forfeit his fellowship.

1878, April 1. Time of payments on account of fellowships.
Resolved, That the payments which may become due in each academic year, on account of the fellowships provided for as above, shall be made in two equal instalments, payable on the fifteenth days of November and May in each year.

SCHOOL OF MINES, BREAKAGE.

1876, June 5. On Reorganizing or Abolishing Department of Breakage.
Resolved, That it be referred to the Committee on the School of Mines to ascertain and report whether the Department "for Breakage and Supplies for Students" of the School of Mines should not be reorganized or abolished.

SCHOOL OF MINES, INSTRUCTION.

1871, March 2. Instruction in School of Mines.
Resolved, That it be referred to a committee to be composed of the Committee on the Statutes and the Committee on the Course, to consider the expediency of discontinuing the Preparatory Class of the School of Mines, and also of making such modification, should any be found necessary, of the studies pursued in the College to the end of the Sophomore year as will give to students at that stage of their course a due preparation to qualify them to enter the School of Mines.

Resolved, That the President be requested to present to the Joint Committee on the Course and the Statutes a copy of the proceedings of the Board in relation to the matters submitted to the Committee regarding the Preparatory Class in the School of Mines, etc.

Resolved, That the following is prescribed as the course of instruction in General Chemistry in the School of Mines:

PREPARATORY CLASS—ELEMENTARY CHEMISTRY.

First Term—Nature and Properties of the Elements and their most important inorganic compounds.

Second Term—Composition of the most usual or most remarkable products of organic nature and their derivatives.

First Year—Regular Students : Theoretical Chemistry.

First Term—Laws of Chemical Combination, embracing the doctrine of Equivalents and the Theory of Atoms, Molecules and Molecular Changes applied to Inorganic Compounds.

Second Term—The same, applied to Organic Compounds.

The course of the Preparatory Class to be so conducted as to prepare the student at its close to enter intelligently upon a course of Qualitative Analysis ; and that of the First Year Class, so as to prepare him similarly to enter upon a course of Quantitative Analysis.

Resolved, Further, that the Professor of General Chemistry be requested to draw up and submit to the Trustees, at their meeting to be held on the first Monday in December next, an outline plan of instruction in accordance with the foregoing principles, embracing the principal topics of instruction in their order ; and that the same, if approved, be hereafter published in the Catalogue of the School. Also,

Resolved, That the Professor of General Chemistry shall, during each term, instruct the students in the whole of the course above allotted to their class for such term, and shall not allow the students of the School of Mines to attend him at the same time with any of the College Classes.

1875, Jan. 4.
Abolition of
Preparatory
Class of School
of Mines. Re-
ferred to Special
Committee.

Resolved, That it be referred to a special committee of five to consider the expediency of abolishing the Preparatory Class of the School of Mines, and if such abolition be deemed by them to be expedient, then to devise and report such modifications of the undergraduate course of instruction as will enable a student to acquire at some stage of that course a due preparation to enter upon such of the courses of the School of Mines as he may select.

1875, May 3.
Students in
Metallurgy to
attend lectures
on Machines.

Resolved, That the students pursuing the course in Metallurgy be required during the three years to attend the lectures on Machines.

1876, Feb. 7.
Instructor in
French to Form
Classes among
Undergraduate
Students, &c.

Resolved, 1. That the Instructor in French of the School of Mines be authorized to form classes among the undergraduate students of the College under such regulations as the Faculty of the College may think proper to establish, and in such hours not already occupied with academic studies as they may chose to assign.

Resolved, 2. That instruction shall actually commence so soon as a number of undergraduate students, not less than fifty, shall have voluntarily enrolled themselves as members of such classes.

Resolved, 3. That the classification shall be made in accordance with the degree of knowledge of the subject which the student shall be found already to possess at the time of enrollment.

Resolved, 4. That the hours given to instruction shall, if practicable, be two per week to each Class, and shall be in any case at least one per week.

Resolved, 5. That after his enrollment in a Class, attendance shall be compulsory upon the student throughout the session for which such Class is formed.

Resolved, 6. That compensation for his services in giving such instruction shall be allowed to the instructor at the rate of five hundred dollars per annum, in addition to his present salary as instructor of the School of Mines, such compensation to be paid in equal instalments at the times at which his present salary becomes due.

1876, June 5.
French and German in School of Mines.

Resolved, That for the more efficient teaching of the French and German Languages, all Classes in the School of Mines to which these languages are taught shall be divided by the Faculty of the School into such sections as may best attain this end consistently with the demands of other portions of the course, and that the instructors in French and German now engaged in teaching in the Classes shall take charge of the sections and receive such increase to their present compensation as may be hereafter determined by this Board.

Resolved, That after the first day of June, 1878, a certain proficiency in the French and German Language (to be hereafter defined and advertised) shall be required for entrance to the School of Mines, such proficiency to be graduated according to the Classes the candidates may propose to enter.

1876, June 5.
Course of Study in the School of Mines.

Resolved, That the course of study in the School of Mines shall continue through four years of time, the years' courses to be called respectively the First, Second, Third and Fourth Classes, and that the use of the term "Preparatory Class" be discontinued, that Class being hereafter known as the First Class.

1876, Dec. 4.
Reference to Committee on School of Mines as to New Chairs of Instruction, etc.

Resolved, That the Committee on the School of Mines be instructed to inquire and report, whether the interests of the School demand the creation of any new chairs of instruction, or any changes in the organization of the Faculty or in the duties of the officers, and that they also inquire and report as to the manner in which these duties are now performed.

1877, April 2.
Reorganization of School of Mines.

For resolutions of this date providing for reorganization of School of Mines—see PROFESSORSHIPS AND PROFESSORS.

1877, May 7.
Resolution referred to Joint Committee of Committee on Statutes and School of Mines

Resolved, That it be referred to a Joint Committee, consisting of the Committees on the Course and the Statutes and the Committee on the School of Mines, to prepare and report at the next meeting of this Board a scheme prescribing the distribution between the different departments of instruction, of time and subject matter in the plan of instruction to be followed till further order in the College and in the School, and also defining the duties of the several members of the Board of the College and the Faculty of the School of Mines, and of all other officers employed in giving instruction in the College or in the School.

1877, June 4. Course of Instruction in School of Mines.

For resolutions of this date as to the course of instruction and the duties of officers, see COURSE OF INSTRUCTION.

1877, Oct. 1. Professor of Engineering to extend Course in Mining and Civil Engineering.

Resolved, That the Professor of Engineering be authorized with the advice and consent of the President, to extend the course of instruction in Mining and Civil Engineering in the Fourth Year into such of the hours assigned to Geodesy and Surveying in that year as can be so employed without prejudice to the instruction in the branches last mentioned.

1878, March 4. Blowpipe analysis optional.

The Scheme of Instruction for the School of Mines, Third Year, Second Session, adopted by this Board, June 4, 1877, was amended so as to read: "Mineralogy Blowpipe Analysis to be optional."

1878, Dec. 2. Resolution on Instruction to be given by the Lecturer on Metallurgy.

Resolved, That the instruction to be given by the Lecturer or non-resident Professor in Metallurgy, for whose appointment provision is made in the resolutions submitted to the Trustees by the Committee on the School of Mines, April 2, 1877, and adopted by the Board, shall consist of a course of lectures on the recent improvements in the manufacture of iron and steel, and the actual state of that manufacture at the present time as regards both theoretical processes and mechanical appliances.

1879, April 7. Volunteer Class in Mechanical Engineering.

Resolved, That the Professor of Engineering be authorized to form a volunteer class from the students of the Fourth Year to pursue a course of practical instruction in Mechanical Engineering in the foundries, machine-shops, and other industrial establishments of the city and vicinity, the same to be approved by the President, and conducted by the Instructor in Mechanical Engineering.

1879, April 7. Additional time in Mechanical Engineering.

Resolved, That instruction in Mechanical Engineering in the Fourth Year be given by the Instructor in that subject one additional hour per week to students in Mining Engineering, and also one additional hour per week to students in Civil Engineering, for the remainder of the term.

1879, April 7.
Students in Civil
Engineering not
to study Analytic Chemistry.

Resolved, That students of Civil Engineering of the Second and Third Classes be not required to study the subject of Qualitative and Quantitative Analysis in Chemistry, but in lieu thereof be required to take all the lectures in General and Applied Chemistry, and on the Metallurgy of iron and steel.

1879, June 2.
School of Mines
Scheme of Studies. Change authorized.

Resolved, That a change be authorized in the Scheme of studies in the School of Mines "by which all engineering students will be required to attend all the lectures in General and Applied Chemistry, and the students in the Chemical Course be required to attend in Geology and Economic Geology."

SERVANTS.

1874, March 2.
Servant for Professor Rood referred to Standing Committee.

Resolved, That the sum of two hundred dollars per annum be allowed to Professor Rood to defray the expenses of a servant to assist him in his Physical Laboratory, to be paid in installments in like manner as the similar allowance to Professor Joy is paid.

1874, Nov. 2.
Benno Kuhnke
appointed Engineer in School
of Mines.

Resolved, That Benno Kuhnke be appointed Engineer of the School of Mines at a salary of one thousand dollars per annum, to hold his position during the pleasure of this Board, with the understanding that he shall perform any duties that may be required of him, and that his appointment take effect from the third day of October last.

1875, March 1.
Professor Newberry to employ boy.

Resolved, That Professor Newberry be authorized to employ a boy in his department at a compensation of not more than five dollars per week, such compensation to date from January 1st, 1874.

1876, Feb. 7.
Resolution authorizing President to pay boy $5 per week.

Resolved, That the amount which, by resolution of January 4th, 1875, the President was authorized to pay as wages of a boy to assist the Janitor be increased from four to five dollars per week, to be given in case, in the judgment of the President, it should be proper to so increase such wages.

1876, Feb. 7.
President to engage Sub-Janitor, $50 per month.

Resolved, That the President be authorized to engage a sub-Janitor for the College, at a compensation not exceeding fifty dollars ($50) a month, and that the Treasurer be authorized to make payment to the person employed to act as sub-Janitor during the month of January past at this rate.

1876, Feb. 7.
President power to remove Sub-Janitor.

Resolved, That it shall be in the power of the President at any time to remove such sub-Janitor for neglect of duty, incompetency, or moral delinquency, and to appoint a suitable person to supply his place.

1878, May 20.
Janitor to remove.

Resolved, That the Janitor remove from his present residence on or before June 1st, next. That the Treasurer be authorized to pay the expenses of his removal and the rent of a house to be hired by him in place of that on the College grounds; provided, however, that the bill for such expenses of removal and the amount of such rent shall be approved by the Standing Committee.

1878, May 20.
Janitor of Law School.

Resolved, That the Janitor shall be appointed by the Committee on the School of Law on the recommendation of the Warden. He to hold his office during the pleasure of the Trustees of the Committee.

1879, Jan. 6.
President to engage an additional Sub-Janitor.

Resolved, That the President be authorized to engage an additional sub-Janitor for the College, at a compensation not exceeding thirty dollars a month, payment to be made from January 1st, 1879.

1879, Jan. 6.
President to remove such Sub-Janitor.

Resolved, That it shall be in the power of the President at any time to remove such additional sub-Janitor for neglect of duty, incompetency, or moral delinquency, and to appoint a suitable person to supply his place.

SPORTS AND GAMES.

1875, April 5.
Appropriation to Sports and Games.

Resolved, That the appropriation to sports and games may be applied to any expenditure approved by the President which will promote and encourage exercises of the students in the open air.

STATUTES.

1874, Dec. 7.
Inquiry on Statutory Provisions School of Mines, Referred to Committee on Statutes.

Resolved, That it be referred to the Committee on Statutes to inquire whether any further statutory provisions are necessary for the regulation of the operation of the School of Mines, and if so to report to the Board such additions to the existing statutes relating to the School, or such substitute for the same, as they may think advisable.

STUDENTS' STUDY-ROOM.

1874, Nov. 2.
Students' Study Room.

Resolved, That the President be authorized to purchase proper books of reference to be placed in the rooms assigned by the Committee on the Site to the use of the students as a study and waiting room.

SYSTEM OF MARKING.

1879. April 7.
Change in the System of Marking for Standing

Resolved, That it be referred to the President and Faculty to devise, if possible, and report to this Board a system of marking to determine the standing of students in the College, less complicated and troublesome than that now in use.

THANKS, RESOLUTIONS OF.

1874, Nov. 2.
Thanks to A. R. Thompson.

Resolved, That the thanks of the Trustees be presented to A. Remsen Thompson, Esq., for his valuable donation to the Library of the College of ancient books, consisting of

Matthews' or Rogers' Bible of 1551.
Sermones Sancti Vincentii.   Lyons, 1493.
La Bible, etc.   Geneve, 1665.
Fulke's Text of the New Testament.   London, 1574.
Newton's System of the World.   London, 1728.
Larcher's Notes on Herodotus.   London, 1844.
Schweighäuser's Herodotus.   Glasgow, 1818.
Anc. Arguments of the Phœnicians.   Pickering.   London, 1832.

Resolved, That a copy of the foregoing resolution be communicated to Mr. Thompson by the Clerk of the Board.

1874, Nov. 2.
Thanks to J.W.
Hamersley   for
Donations.

Resolved, That the thanks of the Trustees be presented to John W. Hamersley, Esq., for the interesting collection of Egyptian curiosities presented by him to the College, and that these objects be suitably arranged in a case by themselves, under the direction of the President, and marked with the name of the donor.

Resolved, That a copy of the foregoing resolution be communicated to Mr. Hamersley by the Clerk of the Board.

1874, Nov. 2.
Thanks to Hon.
Hamilton Fish.

Resolved, That the thanks of the Trustees be presented to the Hon. Hamilton Fish for the valuable donation made by him to the Library of the School of Mines, consisting of an extended and elaborate description of the recently constructed wet and dry docks in the harbor of Marseilles, and the official report to the Government of France of the matters concerning navigation and naval affairs exhibited at the Exposition of 1873 in Vienna.

Resolved, That a copy of the foregoing resolution be communicated to Mr. Fish by the Clerk of the Board.

1874, March 2.
Thanks to S.
L. M. Barlow.

Resolved, That the thanks of the Trustees be presented to Mr. Samuel L. M. Barlow, of this city, for his liberal donation of one thousand dollars made to the department of Mineralogy for the purchase of optical apparatus, and that the Clerk of the Board be requested to transmit a copy of this resolution to Mr. Barlow.

1874, Nov. 2.
Thanks to Prof.
Asa Gray.

Resolved, That the thanks of the Trustees be presented to Professor Asa Gray, Cambridge, Mass, for his liberal donation to the Library of the Herbarium of twenty copies of the report on the botany of the Pacific Coast, contributed by Dr. Torrey to the reports of the Wilkes' exploring expedition, and that a copy of this resolution be communicated to Professor Gray by the Clerk of the Board.

1875, June 7.
Thanks to D.W.
James.

Resolved, That the thanks of the Board of Trustees be given to Mr. D. Willis James for his liberal donation of funds, to the amount of four hundred dollars, for the purchase of instruments for the benefit of the department of Mineralogy in the School of Mines.

Resolved, That a copy of this resolution be communicated to Mr. James by the Clerk of the Board.

1875, June 7.
Thanks to J. J.
Crooke.

Resolved, That the thanks of the Trustees be presented to J. J. Crooke, Esq., for his several generous donations to the Herbarium during the past year, and especially for the munificent gift of the collection of type specimens of plants employed by Mr. A. W. Chapman in the preparation of his "Flora of the Southern United States," purchased by Mr. Crooke at a cost of $2,500.

Resolved, That the foregoing resolution be forwarded to Mr. Crooke by the Clerk of the Board.

1875, Nov. 1.
Thanks to F.
A. Schermer-
horn.

Resolved, That the thanks of the Trustees be given to Mr. F. A. Schermerhorn for the liberal donation of the sum of two thousand francs (2,000 fr.), to be expended in the department of mineralogy and metallurgy in the School of Mines.

Resolved, That the Clerk of the Board be requested to communicate to Mr. Schermerhorn a copy of this resolution.

1876, June 5.
Thanks to A.
R. Thompson.

Resolved, That the thanks of the Trustees be presented to Mr. A. R. Thompson for the generous donation of his valuable collection of minerals to the School of Mines.

Resolved, That a copy of this resolution be transmitted to Mr. Thompson by the Clerk of the Board.

1877, June 4.
Thanks to Chas.
O'Conor.

Resolved, That the thanks of this Board be tendered to the Honorable Charles O'Conor for his excellent address delivered before the graduating class in the Law School on May 16th ; that a copy be respectfully requested for publication.

1877, Oct. 1.
Thanks to S. P.
Davey.

Resolved, That the thanks of the Trustees be presented to Mr. S. P. Davey, of San Francisco, Cal., for his liberal donation to the School of Mines of three flasks of mercury, to be used in the investigation of the loss of heat in furnaces now in progress by the Professor of Metallurgy.

1877, Oct. 1.
Thanks to Coxe
Bros. & Co., and
to others.

Resolved, That the thanks of the Trustees be presented to Messrs. Coxe Bros. & Co., of Drifton, Penn., and especially to Mr. Eckley B. Coxe, of the firm, for their courtesy in admitting the Summer Class of students of the School of Mines to their collieries at Drifton, for the active interest taken by them in the work of the class, for the assistance rendered and facilities afforded them in the prosecution of their object.

Resolved, That this Board further desire to express their sense of obligation to Mr. Arthur McClellan, superintendent of the Cross Creek Collieries, and Messrs. William Powell and Benjamin Gibbon, mining bosses in the same mine, for the personal assistance and instruction kindly rendered by them to the students engaged in practical work in the mines under their direction.

Resolved, That the thanks of the Trustees be presented to the Ebervale Coal Company, at Ebervale, Penn., and particularly to Mr. J. P. McFarlane, superintendent, and Mr. Nesbitt, mining boss, of that mine, for their courteous reception of and kind attention to the students of our School of Mines during their visit to Ebervale in July last.

Resolved, That the thanks of the Trustees be presented to Messrs. Ario Pardee & Co., of Hazleton, Penn., and particularly to Mr. Calvin Pardee, of that firm ; to Mr. Macnair, consulting engineer; and Mr. Thomas Dickenson, mining boss of the Hazleton Mine, for their kind reception of the students of our School of Mines at their visit to Hazleton in July last, and the opportunities afforded to the students to examine the mines.

Resolved, That the thanks of the Trustees be presented to Mr. D. Clark, of Hazleton, for the opportunities kindly afforded the students of our School of Mines to visit and acquaint themselves with the operation of his machine-shop during their visit to Hazleton in July last.

TREASURER.

1874, March 2.
Treasurer to
borrow money.

Resolved, That the Treasurer be authorized to borrow, under the direction of the Standing Committee, a sum not exceeding one hundred and twenty-five thousand dollars, to be applied to the cost of the buildings, alterations, repairs, fixtures and furniture, the construction, making, and purchase of which have been or may be authorized by the Committee on the Site, and also to deliver as security for such loan, under the like direction, the note or notes, bond or bonds of this corporation, under its corporate seal, to be signed by the Clerk.

1875, March 1.
Resolution Authorizing Treasurer to Institute Legal Proceedings, etc.

Resolved, That the Treasurer be authorized, under the direction of the Standing Committee, to institute any legal proceedings for the recovery of any moneys which may at any time be due to the College, or for the enforcement of any right of re-entry reserved by any leases made by the College, and to designate one or more attorneys to conduct any such proceedings, and that the Clerk be authorized to affix the seal of the College to all or any instruments for the appointment of any attorney or attorneys so designated.

1876, Oct. 2.
Resolution authorizing G. M. Ogden to receive award for Fort Washington Ridge Road.

Resolved, That Gouverneur M. Ogden, Treasurer, be authorized to receive the award or awards payable to this corporation, as mortgagees, for land taken for the opening of Fort Washington Ridge road as laid out by the Department of Parks in the City of New York.

1879, March 3.
Treasurer to accept for three years reduced rent, 300 Murray Street.

Resolved, That the Treasurer be authorized to accept for three years, from and after the first day of May next, the rent of $750 per annum for the lot 300 in Murray Street, as in full discharge of the rent renewed for such lot and to accrue during those years.

1879, May 5.
Treasurer authorized to borrow $110,000.

Resolved, That the Treasurer be authorized to borrow from time to time, under the direction of the Standing Committee, a sum not to exceed in the aggregate one hundred and ten thousand dollars, for which the bond or bonds of this corporation shall be issued under its corporate seal.

TUTORSHIPS.

1876, Oct. 2.
Resolution Appointing Tutors in Mathematics and Tutors in Classics.

Resolved, That there be appointed a Tutor in Mathematics to assist in giving instruction in that Department in the College, and also an additional Tutor in Classics; the said officers to receive severally as compensation for their services the salary of twelve hundred dollars ($1,200) per annum, to commence on the 1st of October and to be paid in four equal instalments at the times appointed for the payments of the other College officers.

1877, Dec. 3.
Resolution on
Duty of Tutor
in Rhetoric on
Compositions.

Resolved, That it be made the duty of the Tutor in Rhetoric to examine and criticise such proportion of the English compositions of the Sophomore Class, in addition to those of the Freshman as at present, as in the judgment of the President it shall be necessary to assign him in order to relieve Dr. Schmidt of his present excess of labor.

1877, Dec. 3.
Tutor in Rhe-
toric to be Re-
lieved from In-
structing in
History.

Resolved, Further, that in consequence of the increase of labor thus imposed upon the Tutor in Rhetoric, he is relieved of the duty of giving instruction in History to the Sophomore Class, and that such instruction with that Class be hereafter given by the Professor of the Department of History and Political Science, or by his assistant under his direction.

1879, May 5.
Inquiry as to
Need of Addi-
tional Tutors.

Resolved, That it be referred to the Committee on the Course and Statutes to consider and report whether any additional Tutors will be necessary in the College during the next academic year, and if so, how many and in what Departments.

INDEX.

ACCUMULATING FUND.   PAGE
  Appropriation to, Nov. 1, 1875 7
     "   " Nov. 6, 1876............................... 7
     "   " April 2, 1877....................... 7
     "   " Nov. 5, 1877............................... 7
     "   " June 4, 1877.... 7
ADMISSION—Requirements for, March 1, 1875............... 7
ANNUITY to Prof. Joy, May 7, 1877................................. 8
APPOINTMENTS.
  George Chase, instructor in Law School, Feb. 1, 1875.... 8
  Assistant prof. of municipal law, April 5, 1875 8
  Archibald Alexander appointed, Feb. 5, 1877 8
  R. M. Smith, asst. in history, etc 9
  Prof. of chemistry, May 7, 1877.... 9
  Prof. of engineering, May 7, 1877.... 9
  School of Mines, instructors, June 14, 1877..................... 9, 10
  Registrar of School of Mines, March 4, 1878..................... 9
  Prof. of the law of contracts, etc., April 1, 1878..... 9
  Prof. of medical jurisprudence, May 6, 1878....... 10
  Prof. of constitutional history, etc., May 6, 1878 10
  Prof. criminal law, etc., May 6, 1878 10
  Assistant in geology, May 6, 1878.............................. 10
  Assistants, School of Mines, May 6, 1878 10
  Adjunct prof. in history, etc., June 2, 1878.............. 11
  Lecturer in metallurgy, Dec. 2, 1878............................. 11
APPROPRIATIONS.
  Mechanics, Feb. 2, 1874 11
  Apparatus, April 6, 1874... 11
  Astronomical clock, May 4, 1874........................... 11
  Regulations for, Jan. 4, 1875................................ 11
  Rowing, Dec. 4, 1876......... 12
  Practical mining, June 4, 1877... 13
  For instruction in geodesy and surveying, Nov. 5, 1877............ 13
  For summer class in mining, Feb. 4, 1878..................... 13
  Construction of new building, May 20, 1878.................... . 13
BOARD OF SURVEY.
  To inspect property of the College, Nov. 5, 1877............ 14
  How composed, Nov. 5, 1877......... 14
BOAT HOUSE—Appropriation for, Dec. 7, 1874....................... 14

BUILDINGS.   PAGE
   Houses of profs., Jan, 5, 1874 15
   School of Mines, March 2, 1874 15
   Expenditure approved, Nov. 2, 1874 15
   Consent to hold meetings in, May 3, 1875 15
   Appropriation for, Dec. 6, 1875.......... 15
   Bay window, permission asked for, Nov. 4, 1878............ 16
   Accumulating fund applied to, Jan. 6, 1879 16
CATALOGUE.
   On number of catalogues, May 1, 1876 ....: 16
   Catalogue, number increased, Nov. 5, 1877......................... 16
   Yearly catalogues to contain what, May 6, 1878................... 16
   Catalogue of Law School, May 6, 1878 16
CENTENNIAL EXPOSITION.
   Loan of models, etc., May 1, 1876 17
CLERICAL WORK IN PRESIDENT'S OFFICE.
   President to employ a copying-clerk, March 3, 1879.... 17
   Committee to report as to additional clerk, March 3, 1879.......... 17
CLERK OF BOARD.
   Mr. Halsey for clerk pro tem., June 1, 1874 17
   Clerk pro tem., power of, June 1, 1874.......................... 17
   Resignation of clerk, Nov. 2, 1874 17
   Election of clerk, Nov. 2, 1874 18
COLLEGE OF PHYSICIANS AND SURGEONS.
   Committee on, June 4, 1877 18
   Resolution to dissolve connection, Nov. 4, 1878................... 18
   Conference committee, Nov. 4, 1878 19
COMMITTEES PERMANENT.
   On status of com., etc., Jan. 4, 1875................................. 19
   Resolution on committees, etc., April 5, 1875 19
COMMITTEE ON SITE AND REMOVAL.
   To make contracts, March 2, 1874 19
   Janitor's house to be vacated, March 2, 1874........ 20
   Unforeseen work, compensation for, Nov. 2, 1874.................. 20
   Overcoat, security for, May 3, 1875............................... 20
   Com. on removal, appointment of, Dec. 4, 1876.................... 20
   Expenses to be paid, Jan. 8, 1877................................. 20
   Additional accommodations, Feb. 4, 1878....................... ... 20
   No new buildings to be erected, Feb. 4, 1878..................... . 21
   Report of com. on removal, Feb. 4, 1878......... 21
         "   "   "   Feb. 4, 1878............................. 21
   Plans and estimates for new buildings, April 1, 1878 21
   Expenses of demolition, May 20, 1878............. 21
   Inquiry as to increase of chapel accommodations, Dec. 2, 1878. 21
COMPOSITIONS—Temporary assistants to correct, Oct. 7, 1878.......... 21
DEGREES.
   Case of A. H. Chester, Jan. 5, 1874............... 22
   Proposed extension of rule as to Ph. D., April 6, 1874.............. 22

DEGREES—*Continued.*   PAGE
  Degree of Master of Laws, Dec. 7, 1874............................ 22
  Case of Leonard Waldo, April 5, 1875 22
  Degree Ph. D., requirements for, Jan. 8. 1877. 22
  Degree of Master of Arts, April 1, 1878.. 23
    "   "   " May 6, 1878......... 23
  Non-resident candidates for degree of A. B., March 3, 1879....... 23

EXPENDITURES.
  Regulations governing, Dec. 7, 1874 24
  Expenditures to be made on requisition, April 5, 1875........ 24
  Power of standing committee over, April 5, 1875 24

EXTRA ALLOWANCES.
  Prof. Newberry's application, Jan. 7. 1878........................ 24
  Application of Prof. Newberry granted, Jan. 7, 1878 25
  Extra compensation, rule in regard to, Jan. 7, 1878 25
    "   " to be granted to Prof. Dwight and Prof.
  Chase, Feb 3, 1879 25

FELLOWSHIPS—*See Scholarships and Fellowships.*

FINANCIAL POLICY, Permanent.
  Financial ordinance amended, May 4, 1874.................. 25
  Unexpended balances, May 4, 1874 25
  Amendment to ordinance, May 3, 1875...... 26
  Expenditures for School of Law, May 3, 1875................... .. 26
  Gebhard fund, June 2, 1879........... 26

FORECLOSURE OF MORTGAGES.
  Sale under foreclosure, May 3, 1875...... 26
  Purchase money increased. Nov. 1, 1875 27

FREE TUITION.
  Resolution applied to School of Mines, Feb. 1, 1875 27
  Resolution repealed, June 5, 1876 27
  President's and professors' sons, Dec. 4, 1876..... 27
  Resolutions on free instruction, Dec. 3, 1877.................. 27
    "   "   " April 1, 1878................. 27
    "   "   " April 15, 1878.............. 28

HONORARY Degrees, March 4, 1878..... 28

INSTRUCTION.
  Course of instruction in the College, June 4, 1877...... 30
    "   "   " School of Mines, June 4, 1877......... 32
  Duties of officers, June 4, 1877...................................... 39
  Duties of prof. of history, June 4, 1877...... 47
    "   "   " Oct. 1, 1877........................... .. 47
  Notice required of resolutions affecting course, etc., June 2, 1822 . 47

INSTRUCTION, COURSE OF AND COM. ON THE COURSE.
  Commencement, time of, Jan. 8, 1877.... 48
  Adjunct prof. of philosophy, Jan. 8, 1877 48
  Department of Christian evidences. Feb. 5. 1877..... 48
  Department of charity and correction, Feb. 5, 1877................ 48
  Increase of hours, Feb. 5, 1877................................. ... 48

INSTRUCTION, COURSE OF AND COM. ON THE COURSE—*Continued.*   PAGE
   Oriental languages, Feb. 5, 1877............................ 48
   Prize scholarships, June 4, 1877........................... 48
   Qualifications for admission, May 6, 1878.................. 48
   "   "   "   May 6, 1878..................... 49
   Examinations of schools by Faculty, May 6, 1878........... 49
   Volunteer classes in Greek, May 5, 1879................... 49
   Instruction in Anglo-Saxon, June 2, 1879.................. 49

INSTRUCTION IN MUSIC.
   Cultivation of sacred music, Feb. 5, 1877................. 50
   President to hire piano, Nov. 5, 1877..................... 50
   Dr. Pearce, employment of, Oct. 7, 1878................... 50
   Dr. Walter,   "   " June 2, 1879................ 50

INVENTORY OF MOVABLE PROPERTY.
   Experts to be employed, Nov. 5, 1877...................... 51
LAW SCHOOL—Building, Jan. 7, 1878............................ 51

LAW SCHOOL—DEGREES AND EXAMINATIONS.
   Preliminary inquiry directed, June 1, 1874................ 51
   Degrees, who may be candidates for, June 1, 1874.......... 51
   Examination for admission, Dec. 7, 1874................... 52
   Examination, extent of, Feb. 1, 1875...................... 52
   Examiners, appointed, Feb. 7, 1876........................ 52
   For admission, days of examination fixed, Feb. 7, 1876.... 52
   Bar Association invited to send visitors, Feb. 7, 1876.... 52
   Examiners, how appointed, June 4, 1877.................... 52

LAW SCHOOL—Faculty.
   Existing professorships abolished, April 1, 1878.......... 52
   New professorships established, April 1, 1878............. 53

LAW SCHOOL—Graduation Honors.
   Degree of LL.B., " Cum Laude," April 1, 1878............. 53

LAW SCHOOL—Instruction.
   Course for Master of Laws, Dec. 7, 1874................... 53
   Board to report scheme, May 1, 1876...................... 54
   Warden may assign duties to professors, April 1, 1878.... 54
LAW SCHOOL—Registrar, April 1, 1878......................... 54
LAW SCHOOL—Regulations for support of, April 1, 1878........ 55
LEASES AND RENTS.
   Application of Alvin Higgins, Feb. 2, 1874............... 56
   Mr. Nash's resolution lost, Feb. 2, 1874................. 56
   Standing committee to grant leases, Nov. 2, 1874........ 56
   "   "   "   " Oct. 4, 1875............... 56
   Clerk to affix seal, Oct. 2, 1876........................ 56
   Power to accept surrender of leases, June 5, 1876........ 56
   Clerk to affix seal, June 5, 1876........................ 57
   Surrender of leases, May 7, 1877......................... 57
   "   "   " Nov. 4, 1878......................... 57
   Power to grant renewal, Jan. 5, 1879..................... 57
   On expediency of reducing rents, Feb. 3, 1879............ 57

LEASES AND RENTS—*Continued.* PAGE
Clerk to sign, March 3, 1879.... 57
Rents to be reduced, March 3, 1879............... 57
LEAVE OF ABSENCE.
To H. Newton, Oct. 4, 1875...... 58
To Professor Peck, Jan. 7, 1878........... 58
LIBRARIES.
Life of Johnson to be distributed, March 2, 1874..... 58
Duplicate journals of convention, April 6, 1874.................... 58
Catalogue to be printed, May 4, 1874.............................. 59
Catalogue to be sold, May 4, 1874............................ 59
Library catalogue, distribution of, Nov. 2, 1874 59
Copies of catalogue at disposal of library com., Nov. 2, 1874........ 59
Room for deposit of duplicates, Dec. 7, 1874 59
Compliment to A. R. Thompson, Jan. 4, 1875 59
Copies of catalogue at disposal of committee, March 1, 1875 59
To pay librarian for preparing catalogue, May 3, 1875.............. 59
To print report of librarian, May 3, 1875........................... 59
Committee to dispose of catalogue, June 7, 1875................... 59
On uniting the libraries, Jan. 3, 1876.... 60
Report of library committee on union of libraries, March 6, 1876.... 60
Assistant to librarian of School of Mines, Jan. 3, 1876 60
Libraries of the literary societies, June 5, 1876 60
Librarian and registrar, offices divided, Oct. 1, 1877 60
Appropriation for law library, March 4, 1878.................. 60
On access to library, June 3, 1878................................ 61
Librarian for Law School, Nov. 1, 1878.......................... 61
Superintendence of libraries, Feb. 3, 1879.... 61
LOSS OF COAT.
On loss of coat, June 5, 1876.............................. 61
MINES, SCHOOL OF—*See School of Mines.*
OBSERVATORY.
Appropriation for astronomical clock, May 4, 1874 61
Chronometer for Prof. Peck, Dec. 7, 1874 62
Exact mean solar time, Jan. 3, 1875······· 62
OPTIONAL STUDIES.
As to expediency of optional studies, May 2, 1870................ 62
Arrangements for optional studies, Oct. 3, 1870.... 62
Addition to optional studies, Oct. 1, 1877 63
Chemistry as an optional study, Oct. 1, 1877.......... 63
PRINTING.
Statutes to be printed, Feb. 2, 1874............................ 63
Dr. Haight's address, Feb. 2, 1874 63
Catalogue of library to be printed, May 4, 1874.................... 63
President to print resolutions on expenditures, April 5, 1875........ 63
Expediency of reducing cost of printing, May 3, 1875 63
To print catalogue of School of Mines library, May 3, 1875........ 64
On printing and advertising, Oct 4, 1875........ 64

PRINTING—*Continued.*   PAGE
  Resolution of Faculty as to general catalogue, Nov. 1, 1875 64
  General catalogue to be printed, Nov. 1, 1875 64
  On printing and advertising, Nov. 1, 1875 65
  On publishing advertisements, June 5, 1876........ 65
  Printing questions in Roman antiquities, May 7, 1877 65
  Printing hand-book, etc., May 6, 1878 65
  Stereotype plates for hand-book, Feb. 3, 1879.................... 65

PRIZES.
  Greek prizes, provision amended, May 4, 1874 66
  On prizes in political science, Dec. 6, 1875 66
  Bequest of J. Winthrop Chanler, Jan. 3, 1879 66

PROFESSORSHIPS AND PROFESSORS.
  Assistant in Metallurgy, Feb. 2, 1874 67
  To appoint assistant in physics, May 3, 1875.............. 67
  On chair of history, etc., April 3, 1876 67
  Second assistant in assaying, Dec. 4, 1876 67
  On adjunct professor of philosophy, Feb. 5, 1877....... 67
  The same to hold office three years, Feb. 5, 1877................. .. 67
  Re-organization of the School of Mines, April 2, 1877........... ... 67
  Professors to be appointed for three years, May 7, 1877............. 70
  Adjunct prof. of surveying, etc., to commence July 1, 1877, June 4,
    1877 70
  Instructor in mechanical engineering, June 4, 1877............. ... 70
  Title of assistant in drawing, June 4, 1877 71
  Term of service of adjunct profs., instructors, etc., June 4, 1877 . 71
  Assistant to prof. of history, Oct. 1, 1877. 71
  On use of official title by professors, May 6, 1878.................. 71
  Adjunct prof. of history, June 3, 1878............................. 72

PUBLIC WORSHIP.
  On public worship, Nov. 6, 1876..................................... 72
  On appointment of roll-officers, Feb. 5, 1877 72
  President to appoint additional roll-officers, March 3, 1879. 72

REPAIRS AND ALTERATIONS.
  President to audit bills for past repairs, May 3, 1875.....: 73
  President to direct small repairs, June 7, 1875...................... 73
  Standing committee to employ architect, June 7, 1875 73
  Room to be prepared for duplicates of library, June 7, 1875........ 73
  Action of committee in vacation confirmed, Oct. 4, 1875 73
  President's power as to repairs extended, Dec. 6, 1875 73
  Inquiry as to storeroom of School of Mines, June 5, 1876........... 74
  Chapel to be enlarged, June 4, 1877 74
  Room to be prepared for professor of geology, Nov. 5, 1877 74
  Inquiry as to sufficiency of heating apparatus, April 1, 1878........ 74
  Additional seats to be placed in chapel, Jan. 6, 1879 74

RESIGNATION.
  On resignation of Mr. Rutherfurd, Jan. 8, 1877.... 74

SALARIES.
                                                                     PAGE
  Prof. Joy's salary increased, Jan. 5, 1874 75
  Salary of assistant to professor of astronomy, April 5, 1875 75
  Of assistant professor of municipal law, Nov. 1, 1875 75
  Salaries of professors hereafter, Feb. 7, 1875 75
  Foregoing resolutions to take effect, Feb. 7, 1875 76
  On salary of professor of history, etc., May 1, 1876 76
  Salaries of instructors in French and German, Nov. 6, 1876 76
SCHOLARSHIPS AND FELLOWSHIPS.
  Scheme of scholarships reported, April 3, 1871 76
  Scheme of fellowships reported, April 3, 1871 77
  Resolutions on above schemes, April 3, 1871 78
  Inquiry as to conditions of fellowships, Nov. 2, 1874 78
  Division of scholarships not permitted, Nov. 1, 1875 79
  Schermerhorn free scholarships founded, April 2, 1877 79
  Sophomore scholarship in chemistry, April 2, 1877 79
  Provisions relating to fellowships repealed, April 1, 1878 79
  Mode of conferring fellowships, April 1, 1878 79
  Fellows to pursue course of study, etc., April 1, 1878 80
  Payment on account of fellowships, April 1, 1878 80
SCHOOL OF MINES—Breakage, June 5, 1876 80

SCHOOL OF MINES—INSTRUCTION.
  On discontinuing preparatory class, March 2, 1874 80
  Proceedings as to preparatory class, April 6, 1874 81
  General chemistry, Nov. 2, 1874 81
  On expediency of abolishing preparatory class, Jan. 4, 1875 82
  Students in metallurgy to attend lectures on machines, May 3, 1875. 82
  On instruction in French to undergraduates, Feb. 7, 1876 82
  Sections for study of French and German, June 5, 1876 82
  French and German required for admission, June 5, 1876 83
  Course of study four years, June 5, 1876 83
  Inquiry as to new chairs of instruction, Dec. 4, 1876 83
  Reorganization of school, April 2, 1877 83
  Joint committee of inquiry as to scheme, May 7, 1877 83
  Course of engineering extended, Oct. 1, 1877 84
  Blowpipe analysis optional, March 4, 1878 84
  Lectures on metallurgy, course defined, Dec. 2, 1878 84
  Volunteer class in mechanical engineering, April 7, 1879 84
  Additional time in mechanical engineering, April 7, 1879 84
  Students in civil engineering not to study analytical chemistry,
    April 7, 1879 85
  Change in scheme of studies, June 2, 1879 85
SERVANTS.
  Boy for Prof. Rood, March 2, 1874 85
  Appointment of Benno Kulmke as Engineer, Nov. 2, 1874 85
  Boy for Prof. Newberry, March 1, 1875 85
  Increase of pay to sub-janitor, Feb. 7, 1876 85
  President to engage sub-janitor, Feb. 7, 1876 86

SERVANTS—*Continued.*   PAGE
    President power to remove sub-janitor, Feb. 7, 1876 86
    Janitor's residence, May 20, 1878........ 86
    Janitor of Law School, May 20, 1878 86
    President to engage additional sub-janitor, Jan. 6, 1879 86
    President power to remove sub-janitor, Jan. 6, 1879................ 86
SPORTS AND GAMES.
    Appropriations, how to be applied, April 5, 1875................. .. 86
STATUTES.
    Inquiry on statutory provisions for School of Mines, Dec. 7, 1874... 87
STUDENTS' STUDY-ROOM.
    President authorized to purchase books, Nov. 2, 1874 87
SYSTEM OF MARKING FOR STANDING, April 7, 1879................... 87
THANKS, RESOLUTIONS OF.
    To A. R. Thompson, Nov. 2, 1874................. 87
    To J. W. Hamersley, Nov. 2, 1874......... 88
    To Hon. Hamilton Fish, Nov. 2, 1874............................. 88
    To S. L. M. Barlow, March 2, 1874 88
    To Prof. Asa Gray, Nov. 2, 1874 88
    To D. W. James, June 7, 1875 88
    To J. J. Crooke, June 7, 1875 89
    To F. A. Schermerhorn, Nov. 1, 1875 89
    To A. R. Thompson, June 5, 1876 89
    To Charles O'Conor, June 4, 1877 89
    To S. P. Davey, Oct. 1, 1877 89
    To Messrs. Coxe Bros. & Co. and others, Oct. 1, 1877............... 89
TREASURER.
    To borrow money, March 2, 1874....... 90
    To institute legal proceedings, March 1, 1875.................... . 91
    Authorized to receive award, Oct. 2, 1876........... 91
    To accept reduced rent, March 3, 1879............................ 91
    To borrow money, May 5, 1879 91
TUTORSHIPS.
    Tutorship in mathematics established, Oct. 2, 1876................ 91
    Duty of tutor in rhetoric, Dec. 3, 1877............... 92
    Tutor in rhetoric to be relieved, Dec. 3, 1877....... 92
    Additional tutors, May 5, 1879 92